about Relevant Ministry, Inc.

W0010616

Relevant Ministry is a biblically-based, interdenominational ministry that equips leaders and empowers individuals to minister relevantly in healthy and thriving churches.

Being located on the Mississippi Gulf Coast, Hurricane Katrina was the catalyst for RM's ministry to churches. Pam and I moved to Gulfport, Mississippi in 2004 to pastor a church just before Katrina ravaged the area in 2005. Like everyone who experienced this storm, we rolled up our sleeves and got involved in the physical rebuilding. Three years later, we were exhausted; and, other leaders and churches were experiencing the same post-hurricane symptoms. Then in 2008, we started Relevant Ministry around a healthy church initiative with the purpose of spiritual rebuilding and revitalization.

As we ministered to church leaders, a deficiency around discipleship continued to be a topic of significant concern for most churches. As a result, a discipleship process that is both relevant and field tested was developed.

In the process of developing the Relevant Discipleship Pathway™ the goal was to answer two major questions..."How could discipleship be an intentional, ongoing, transformational process?" And, "How could a discipleship process truly multiply, where disciples make disciples who make disciples?"

The outcome is the Relevant Discipleship Pathway™ inspired by the chronological stages of Jesus' ministry with the coaching approach empowering spiritual conversations with others. Relevant Discipleship™ is an intentional discipleship process immersing believers into biblical disciplines leading to a transformed life in Jesus Christ.

From the beginning in 2008, and our over forty years of ministry experience, Relevant Ministry now trains and helps implement the tried and proven pathway process of discipleship with a coaching approach in churches in the United States and around the world.

about the cover of the book

When I was in high school, back in the mid-1960's, the church youth group I was part of experienced Lyman Coleman's Bible study, Acts Alive. If you are familiar with Lyman Coleman, you know he's regarded as the modern-day pioneer of the small group movement.

On our family farm there was a 'seed house,' and that's where we held our gatherings for this study. The 'seed house' provided the perfect atmosphere for our gatherings, and if I remember correctly, we called them 'hootenannies.' Wow, I'm really dating myself! We sang folk songs and listened to lessons; but, the primary emphasis was on having an open mic and audience participation. What made our youth group gatherings special was how Lyman Coleman's lessons gave space for serendipitous moments.

The cover of this book is a depiction of a drawing I drew from one of the Acts Alive lesson assignments. I was impacted by the passage in Luke 5:11, "So they pulled their boats up on shore, left everything and followed him." Back in the 60's, I remember the night I shared my drawing titled, "Their Beached Boat" saying, "I was challenged by the commitment of those followers of Jesus." The disciples left it all to follow Jesus.

I'm thankful for my church youth leaders who laid a solid foundation for me to become a follower. And thank you, Lyman Coleman, for your influence on my life and in my ministry.

endorsements

I found the Relevant Discipleship Pathway so powerful and life giving. The discipleship resources are both interesting and thought provoking.

—Rev. Kim Alexander
Horison Methodist Church
Johannesburg, South Africa

Discipleship Coaching and engaging in the Relevant Discipleship Pathway has brought me back to the basics.

—Rev. DeeDee Autry, PCC, Senior Pastor
Mountainside United Methodist Church
Hot Springs Village, AR

The Relevant Discipleship Pathway has become a lifesaver for me. My frustration has been with programs and classes that produce smarter Christians; yet, not necessarily mature believers.

—Bil Barkley, LPC
Minister of Education and Senior Adults
First Baptist Church
Mount Pleasant, TX

The Relevant Discipleship Pathway has been a tremendous catalyst in my spiritual growth. It was a challenging, enjoyable journey that continues to this day. The relational component along with the coaching emphasis, motivated and encouraged me along the way.

—Kevin Beachy, Lead Pastor
Gulf Coast Church
Long Beach, MS

I just wanted to let you know how helpful the Relevant Discipleship Pathway and our one-to-one discipleship coaching sessions have been for me and for my time to plan discipleship in our church.

—Adam L. Brice, Pastor
Resurrection Presbyterian Church
West Lafayette, IN

I want to share about Relevant Discipleship and about the 7 disciplines. From the time I started discipleship one-to-one, with my brother Jesse McBride, many things started to change in my life.

—Ramon Hernan Castellanos, Pastor
San Felipe Church
San Felipe, Orange Walk, Belize

I'm excited about what is happening in my church around discipleship. I can imagine all of our Garifuna churches implementing Relevant Discipleship.

—Pedro Castro, Discipleship Overseer
Evangelical Garifuna Church
New Orleans, LA

The Relevant Discipleship Pathway, along with the one-to-one disciple-making process utilizing the Nehemiah Response Coaching Model was the missing ingredient and the perfect complement to the group discipleship opportunities already taking place in the faith community I serve.

—Rev. Wayne H. Clemens
Centerpoint Christian Fellowship Church
Barneveld, NY

The Relevant Discipleship Pathway has helped me to become more aware of two paths of discipleship...being a disciple myself, growing into the likeness and image of Jesus Christ; and, being a disciple maker.

—Commander Daneck Dang-awan
Military Chaplain, Armed Forces of the Philippines
Manila, Philippines

The Relevant Discipleship Pathway was the nudge I needed to go back to seven basic themes that should be a part of every Christ follower.

—Bob Depew, Pastor
Way of Life Community Church
Mobile, AL

While I have been deeply committed to the practice of discipleship throughout my ministry, I have also been frequently disappointed in the various methods and materials I've used. Discipleship Coaching has changed that! I am walking into the next ministry season invigorated and filled with anticipation of seeing disciples making disciples!

—Joe Donaldson
Associate Pastor and Discipleship Coach
Journey Church
Federal Way, WA

The intentional, transformational process of the Relevant Discipleship Pathway is unique because it uses a coaching approach; which, produces a relational process where we grow to become more like Jesus.

—Justus Froman, Lead Pastor
Bayou Talla Fellowship
Kiln, MS

I finally came to the realization that God was transforming me by the 'renewing of my mind.' I get it! And the transformation came through the Relevant Discipleship Pathway and experiencing Discipleship Coaching.

—Julie Gallagher-Gough, ACC
Keller, TX

Even though I have been a Christian for 35 years, Discipleship Coaching challenged me to take my spiritual journey to another level.

—Tom Granoff, Ph.D., PCC
Dissertation Statistician / Methodologist /
Professor
Pepperdine University
Malibu, CA

The Relevant Discipleship Pathway focuses on the disciplines of a disciple and inviting God to open up my understanding and my connection to Him. The pathway, coupled with my regular coaching conversations with Nelson, led to some amazing shifts in my heart and a deeper connection to the Almighty God.

—Jeff Harmon
New Apostolic Church
Brilliance Within Coaching and Consulting
Parsippany, NJ

I greatly appreciate the theology of the Relevant Discipleship Pathway and Discipleship Coaching, as it is extremely balanced.

—Dr. David P. Hyatt, PCC
Effective Ministries Coaching and Consulting
St. Louis, MO

Every time Nelson and I engaged in the Relevant Discipleship Pathway together, I was greatly encouraged and sharpened in my own relationship with Jesus and eager to coach others in a disciple-making way of life. You hold helpful and encouraging material in your hands!

—Erik Johnson
Pastor of Worship and Disciplemaking
Crosspoint Community Church
Eureka, IL

Becoming involved and discipled in the methods of the Relevant Discipleship Pathway has personally opened up the movement of the Holy Spirit, and put breath into how we are to live in relationship with God and all others in the world.

—Jenn Klein, Pastor
Hamilton United Methodist Church
Hamilton, MO

My experience with the Relevant Discipleship Pathway has given me a new way to engage in discipleship; providing friendship, fellowship, and resources for both personal and congregational growth.

—Philip McMurrin, Pastor
Pastor, Concord United Methodist Church
Brooksville, KY
Chaplain, Hospice of Hope
Maysville, KY

Walking an intentional, inquisitive journey of discovery into a new reality of Christ. This describes the transforming experience I discovered with Relevant Discipleship.

—Rev. Lilian Reyneke
Methodist Church of South Africa
Orkney Society South Africa

What I found in the Relevant Discipleship Pathway is a discipleship pathway that actually has potential for making and multiplying disciples.

—Phyllis Riney, D. Min., PCC
Discipleship Coach
Texas Conference UMC
Houston, TX

In my two decades of ministry I have experienced various forms of discipleship training but none that compares to Relevant Discipleship. The well developed training provides a clear and concise pathway to discipleship, significant resources, and a transformational coaching model. The one-to-one coaching not only strengthened the core aspects of discipleship in my life, but helped me in implementing a flourishing discipleship process within my ministry.

—Dr. Abe Smith, Minister
First United Methodist Church
Allen, TX

What makes Relevant Discipleship unique is the coaching approach that is used. Although the excellent resources are relatable to any believer, the Relevant Discipleship one-to-one process is customized for the individual on his or her personal, spiritual journey. In addition, the intentional process takes one beyond awareness to actual steps and actions that lead to real transformation!

—Len Thebarge, Senior Associate Pastor
Grace Church
Normal, IL

I was immensely impressed when I learned about the Relevant Discipleship Pathway. The content includes a deep dive into the discipleship process and how to systematise the introduction of such processes into one-to-one work.

—Richard Thorby ACC, MBA (IMD)
Matrix Consulting UK Ltd, Executive Coach
Horsham, England, UK

The Relevant Discipleship Pathway gave me the tools for deeper conversations and the experience of coaching others. As a coach, I was already familiar with the techniques of deep listening, powerful questions, and action and accountability. However, I had been using those tools primarily for programs, not for strengthening a person's relationship to God.

—Rev. Marilyn Wadkins
T.E.A.M. Ministries
Houston, TX

The Relevant Discipleship Pathway is a descriptive way of understanding how each person is invited to move from viewing faith to abiding in God's presence. And yet, that's not the final chapter. The pathway leads us into the presence of God, transforms and sends us forth to minister to others.

—Rena Yocom
Missiologist, Theological educator, and
Retired clergy in UMC
Edgerton, KS

RELEVANT DISCIPLESHIP
PATHWAY

RELEVANT DISCIPLESHIP
PATHWAY

...a framework for intentional transformation
and multiplication

Nelson Roth, PCC
forward by Dr. Bob Logan

Relevant Ministry Publishing
Gulfport, MS, United States

ISBN-13: 978-0692182208
ISBN-10: 0692182209

Relevant Ministry Publishing
Gulfport, MS
United States

www.relevantministry.org

dedication

My wife, Pam, is both an encourager and example for me. Over our 50 plus years together, in both life and ministry, she has been a faithful supporter. And, as I write about discipleship, I find her on every page of this book beautifully illustrating what it means to be a follower of Christ; as a wife, mother, grandmother, great-grandmother, daughter, sister, and friend. Pam, to you I dedicate this book. Thank you for your encouragement and example.

Nelson Roth
Co-founder of Relevant Ministry, Inc.

contents

foreward   21

introduction   25

1   what is discipleship   29

2   what to do   39

3   what to say   51

4   first things first   63

5   practicing the 7 disciplines   77

6   the outcome, ongoing transformation   93

7   the Holy Spirit   111

8   resources to get started   127

9   making room to experience God   137

10   multiplication   153

what's next   171

appendix   175

notes   181

bibliography   185

glossary   189

resources   199

foreward

I first met Nelson Roth in New Orleans after he'd been involved in Hurricane Katrina. He had a passion for the needs of people and very much the heart of a servant. Nelson was also committed to long-term cleanup and rebuilding from the effects of Katrina. He'd been involved in addressing physical needs for a long while and was just then transitioning to spiritual needs as well. I had the privilege of coaching him during that season.

Nelson truly understood that we can also help people put their lives back together from the vantage point of the spiritual realm. His ministry took on a strong discipleship focus: intentional, transformational, and multiplying. As a true Barnabas-type, Nelson has a good heart for people and truly loves seeing others released to their fullest potential. He understands that taking a coaching approach is a powerful way to do that. He's a come-alongside kind of guy who truly wants to empower people: a practitioner who really practices discipleship in an other-centered kind of way.

To give you an idea, one of Nelson's many gems from *Relevant Discipleship Pathway* is this one:

> I'm continually amazed how repeatedly people come up with creative solutions and plans when the coaching approach is used in the discipleship session. The coaching approach allows the person being discipled an opportunity to express what they have been thinking, and to be validated in the process. Through the process, the person being discipled takes ownership of the plan because it fits best at that time with their situation and style. Otherwise, the tendency, without a coaching approach, might be to prescribe or impose a particular solution that we may think would work best. Unfortunately, nearly without fail, this is not the best approach.

In addition to his emphasis on vital coaching and listening skills, Nelson takes a solidly practical approach to discipleship, addressing the critical questions of "what to do" and "what to say" in discipling relationships. Nelson draws from his extensive pastoral and coaching experience to bring you two very practical tools for discipleship: The Relevant Discipleship Pathway and The Nehemiah Response Coaching Model. Both of them address the question, "How?" that is so often neglected when discussing the topic of discipleship.

Lots of people can talk theory and theology all day. They can preach sermons on the "whys" and the "shoulds" of discipleship. But this book gives you actual tools you can put into use. As Nelson says, "Discipleship is not a curriculum to complete, but a way of life for the rest of your life."

Eminently readable and firmly rooted in scripture, *Relevant Discipleship Pathway* gives people rails to run on. His approach is structured—3 Rs, 7 Disciplines—yet fully Spirit-led and coaching-oriented. Nelson asks questions to the reader throughout, helping us reflect on our own contexts, our own discipleship journeys, as well as our discipling of others.

This book is a product of a person who truly does—in the words of Henry Blackaby—find out where God is working and join him there. This kind of approach to discipleship—and life—will lead you to the next thing and then the next thing and then the next thing. So take it to heart and live it out.

Dr. Bob Logan
Logan Leadership
Author of *The Discipleship Difference* and
Becoming Barnabas

introduction

A couple of years ago, our grandson, who lives 800 miles from us, and I were personally experiencing the discipleship pathway you will learn about in this book. We were intentionally connecting regularly with a video call; but then, life got in the way, and the discipleship sessions were on hold. After several months of not connecting, we were able to spend a few days together. During a conversation one day, he expressed feeling guilty and was apologetic about not continuing to stay connected for our one-to-one discipleship sessions.

Hearing him verbalize his disappointment of needing to put discipleship on hold because of his busy schedule, I said, "It's okay," and continued to encourage him by saying, "we all go through different seasons in our life." I went on to explain the Relevant Discipleship Pathway™ isn't a curriculum to complete; instead, ultimately we include the practice of discipleship throughout our life. At that moment, there was a long pause in our conversation; and then, I saw a smile on his face as he began to respond with an incredible realization. "So, I get it! Discipleship is a way of life for the rest of your life." That phrase, "a way of life for the rest of your life" stuck with me that day; and, that's exactly what this book is all about!

> *Discipleship is a lifelong journey. It's not a curriculum to complete. It's a way of life for the rest of your life. @nelsonroth*

So, if you hunger for a more in-depth relationship with Jesus that's intentional, you're holding in your hands a book that could be transformational for you. Our prayer is you will discover something unique and fruitful in this book.

Two key aspects set Relevant Discipleship™ apart from other discipleship curriculums or programs ...the Relevant Discipleship Pathway™ and the Nehemiah Response Coaching Model™. As you are experiencing the Relevant Discipleship Pathway™, you will learn a unique system or framework for intentional transformation which leads to the multiplication of disciples. And, the Nehemiah Response Coaching Model™ will equip you with three useful coaching techniques. With these two key aspects in place, we have also designed a resource manual...*Relevant Discipleship™ Resource Manual* filled with articles, coaching tools and lessons to equip you to first of all experience being a disciple and then to become a disciple maker.

> *Discipleship is a transformational process that takes time. It challenges our consumer mentality that 'the next big event' is our solution. @nelsonroth*

What does God want us to do? Before we get into chapter one, let's take a look at a significant statement by Aubrey Malphurs.

> Perhaps the most important questions that the church and its leadership can ask are: What does God want us to do? What is our mission? What are our marching orders? The answers are not hard to find. More than two thousand years ago, the Savior predetermined the church's mission. It's the Great Commission, as found in such texts as Matthew 28:19–20; Mark 16:15; Luke 24:46–49; John 20:21; and Acts 1:8. [1]

1 what is discipleship

John the Baptist launched Jesus' public ministry when he said, "Look, the Lamb of God, who takes away the sin of the world" (John 1:29, 36). Shortly after, Jesus was baptized, tested in the wilderness, and then he began to preach. Around four to five months after his baptism, Jesus invited some of the disciples of John who were curious to "Come, ...and you will see" (John 1:39). Along the way, around ten to eleven months after his baptism, Jesus said to Peter and his brother Andrew; and James and John, "Come, follow me, and I will send you out to fish for people" (Matthew 4:19 and Mark 1:17).

Being and Making

Notice Jesus' call found in Matthew 4, and Mark 1 is in two-parts..."follow me" and "fish for people." It is imperative to understand this two-part call as we consider what discipleship is all about...'being a disciple' and 'making disciples.' And, it is important to realize this call to follow him happened ten to eleven months into Jesus' three-year ministry.

"So then, what is discipleship?" As you consider your answer to this question, how beneficial is it for you to know Peter and Andrew; and James and John's response to Jesus' invitation to be a follower was a process? These four men didn't unquestionably leave their nets or their father alone in the boat the first time they met Jesus; instead, there was possibly a natural hesitation, a reasonable counting of the cost; and yet, they were curious about this man called Jesus. Ultimately, Peter, Andrew, James, and John became committed disciples, followers of Christ.

At best, we can only speculate that curiosity about this man called Jesus may have preceded the

> Discipleship is a passionate devotion to a person—our Lord Jesus Christ. What does following Him look like for you? @nelsonroth

commitment of these four men to accept the call. How does this timeline impact you seeing discipleship as a process, a lifelong journey? For now, keep that thought in the back of your mind as we will consider more fully the chronological timeline of Jesus' ministry in the next chapter.

What is your understanding of Jesus' first request to 'follow me' as a disciple? How much is Jesus emphasizing to us as he did to Peter, Andrew, James, and John, you must 'be something' before you 'do something?' Here's a thought to consider...what if the 'follow me' is all about growing instead of going? Peter, Andrew, James, and John needed to 'grow' as disciples of Jesus before they could 'go.' Jesus had a plan; and he was looking for committed followers who would leave their fishing nets, grow in their spiritual walk first and then go out willingly to fish for people as he had commissioned them to do.

Defining Discipleship

At this point, how would you define being a Christian disciple? According to *Vine's Expository Dictionary of New Testament Words*, the word disciple means 'a learner' and 'one who follows one's teaching.' [1]

Dallas Willard says, "Spiritual formation is a process that happens to everyone...Terrorists, as well as saints, are the outcome of spiritual formation. Their spirits or hearts have been formed." [2] Alan Hirsch in *The Forgotten Ways*, says something similar. "If we don't disciple people, the culture sure will." [3]

So, a fully committed believer in Christ who desires to learn more about him, to follow him, and become like him, is a Christian disciple. Evidently, this is precisely what God intended. Paul wrote in Romans 8:29, "For those God foreknew he also predestined to be conformed to the image of his Son..." Likewise, Jesus said in Luke 6:40, "...everyone who is fully trained will be like their teacher."

George Barna has this to say about being a fully devoted follower, "What would happen for God's kingdom if we did not consider our job complete when people confess their sins and say a prayer inviting Jesus to be their Redeemer, but would use their new commitments to Christ as a launching pad for a lifelong quest to become individuals who are completely sold out – emotionally, intellectually, physically, spiritually – to the Son of God?" [4]

My wife, Pam, and I have written and teach a coach training course called Certificate in Discipleship Coaching. One of the assignments in the class is for each student to write a definition of what discipleship means to them personally. Here is a definition from one of the students. "A disciple commits to a lifetime of knowing Christ, growing in Christ, serving Christ, and sharing Christ with the world."

Pause and Ponder

Where are you on the pathway as far as being a Christian disciple? Still curious?
If you're a believer, how committed are you?
How would you define discipleship?

Marks of a Disciple

So then, if growing as a Christian disciple comes first in this process of following Christ, how can we know we're developing or maturing? John the disciple helps us with this question by identifying three specific pieces of evidence that give proof we are his disciples..."hold to his teaching" in John 8, "to love one another" in John

13, and "to bear fruit" found in John 15. Some questions you might want to ask yourself are..."How do I see these three pieces of evidence or characteristics of Christ in my life?" Or, "What's my desire to see these three characteristics become more predominant in my life?"

First, John gave us a clear expression of what it 'really' means to be a disciple when he recorded Jesus' words in John 8:31, "If you hold to my teaching, you really are my disciples." What does this statement mean to you to "hold" to Jesus' words?

Let's take a moment here to look at James 1:22. How does this verse help us to answer the question above..."What does it mean to hold to Jesus' words?" You might want to prepare yourself because this verse is pretty clear in the fact that we have a responsibility in this whole thing called discipleship. James 1:22 reads, "Do not merely listen to the word, and so deceive yourselves. Do what it says." Ouch! You mean discipleship asks for my obedience?

> Discipleship is following Christ on his terms not ours. What changes does that mean for you?
> @nelsonroth

Before we look at the second and third characteristic of a disciple, let's stop to read a personal story about obedience from a disciplee experiencing the Relevant Discipleship Pathway™. This person ended up practicing the verse in James 1:22 and discovered the benefits of obedience.

Solitaire – keeps the brain engaged; harmless and fun! Right? Well, I believed that. At least until the day, I realized I had been playing Solitaire on my phone for well over two hours straight.

For several months, I had been working through the spiritual disciplines of the Relevant Discipleship Pathway™. On the day of the Solitaire marathon, I was working on the discipline of Discipleship: growing godly in character with a foundation of personal values and purpose.

It was then, I realized the Solitaire app had to go from my phone. I would like to say, "I joyfully deleted the app;" but, that would not be truthful. Instead, it took prayer and grit because I was addicted to playing the game whenever I had ANY amount of downtime.

When I finally hit 'delete' on the Solitaire app, I experienced freedom and lightness. And then, I was reminded of one of the articles in the resource manual for the 'Discipleship' discipline…"Jesus does not ask for a little bit, or even a lot from us….he asks for ALL." I believe that includes letting go/getting rid of something as seemingly insignificant as being hooked on Solitaire.

So far, we've seen the importance of 'holding' to Jesus' words explained as obedience in the Scripture reference in the book of James. And through a personal story from someone on the discipleship pathway, we have heard how obedience is an essential element to having this characteristic in our life. Now, in John 13:35, we learn the second evidence, "...everyone will know that you are my disciples, if you love one another." How does the thought of loving one another challenge you?

The third and last evidence in the list of characteristics of a disciple is found in John 15 when Jesus is giving final instructions before he goes to the cross. In verse eight, where John uses the analogy of the vine and the branches, we read, "This is to my Father's glory, that you bear much fruit, showing yourselves to be my disciples." How much are you producing spiritual fruit in your life? (see Galatians 5:22-23)

So in summary, personal growth of the discipleship process can be known by these three specific pieces of evidence.

- Holding to Christ's teaching
- Loving others
- Bearing much fruit

As we wrap up this chapter, how are you doing in the areas of holding to Christ's teachings, loving others and bearing much fruit? Which of these three characteristics of maturity as a disciple of Christ would you like to grow in more?

One of the hindrances for not engaging in discipleship we hear all of the time is, "I don't know what to do." What to do, as far as being a disciple; and also, how to disciple another person.

How does a person get on a pathway of 'growing' and 'going;' and what is the next step? As we saw earlier, 'doing' follows 'being.' Let's discover the action steps to take in the next chapter.

what leaders are saying…

> The Relevant Discipleship Pathway has helped me to become more aware of two paths of discipleship…being a disciple myself; growing into the likeness and image of Jesus Christ; and, being a disciple maker. I had the opportunity to experience one-to-one discipleship with Nelson. These sessions have helped me on my own discipleship journey.
>
> —Commander Daneck Dang-awan
> Military Chaplain, Armed Forces of
> the Philippines
> Manila, Philippines

> The Relevant Discipleship Pathway impacted me personally by having someone there who cared enough about my spiritual growth to connect with me one-to-one, providing accountability in an environment where I could be real about my walk with Christ. The intentional, transformational process of the Relevant Discipleship Pathway is unique because it uses a coaching approach; which, produces a relational process where we grow to become more like Jesus. Rather than a program to complete, it is a lifestyle of making disciples. Our vision is to multiply discipleship out within the context of our

church by utilizing Relevant Discipleship to connect new believers and new members into a relationship with a discipler.

—Justus Froman, Lead Pastor
Bayou Talla Fellowship
Kiln, MS

2 what to do

Someone once referred to me as being 'systemic' long before I fully understood the meaning of the word in the context of an organization like the church. Our church was close in proximity to a Christian University and Seminary, so a professor who was familiar with our ministry asked if we would be interested in supplying an intern from their grad program with a position for the summer. While on a routine visit to our church to evaluate the grad student on her roles and responsibilities, the professor began making observations about how I interacted with the intern and some of the ways we operated in our ministry as a whole. At the end of his evaluation of the intern, he commented on how I was a systemic leader. And then, he went on to explain how systemic leaders relate to a group or a system as it affects the whole of the organization...not to be confused with being methodical. Wow! I was blown away by the fact that something as important as an organizational operating system seemed to come naturally for me. That was a significant realization and helped to define my ministry leadership style.

Since then, I've incorporated this leadership style knowing that a church is not a place dominated by separate, unrelated forces. To be a healthy church, all systems must be operating effectively, and when they are, there will be life and growth. Like nature or our human bodies, there are visible and invisible interrelated 'actions' that affect the different systems for the good or not so good. It's the same way for the church. How much do we limit health, growth, or change because we compartmentalize the various systems that can better complement and complete each other when they function together?

Think about it, if the church is a body, a systems approach to leading makes incredible sense. So let's begin to look at discipleship as a lifelong, interrelated system or process.

Pause and Ponder

What are the integral elements of discipleship?
How can these elements be integrated, working together to accomplish the overall goal?

Core Aspects of Discipleship

Relevant Discipleship™ and its pathway consists of several interrelated parts that breathe life and health into a disciple's lifelong journey. Once on the pathway, a believer grows as a disciple of Christ and then becomes a disciple maker. To summarize, the Relevant Discipleship Pathway™ is a framework for intentional transformation and multiplication!

To represent Relevant Discipleship™, we have developed a graphic you will find in the Appendix on page 175. As I describe this graphic, refer to the image and notice the three concentric circles, with God in the center...the inside circle. The 3Rs...relationship, responding, and revealing Christ are at the core of the middle circle; and, the 7 Disciplines of a disciple make up the outer circle. The second graphic in the Appendix on page 176 has arrows overlaid representing the pathway as the inward and outward journey. The arrows note six significant stages of reference embodying Christ's ministry which we will define beginning in the next paragraph. So with the two graphics in mind, the 7 Disciplines of a disciple flow inward, making room to experience God. And then, flow outward from the center bringing transformation in our lives around the 3Rs ... relationship, responding, and revealing Christ.

> Discipleship is a process not a program. If that's true, how does it change the way you experience discipleship? @nelsonroth

It is important to note here the Relevant Discipleship Pathway™ follows the chronological timeline of Jesus' ministry. Let's consider how Jesus interacted with his disciples. A historical study of events comparing all four Gospels determines the chronological timeline of events used in the Relevant

Discipleship Pathway™. The Gospels of Matthew, Mark, Luke, and John record the events of Jesus' ministry and can be viewed together for both similarities and differences. Each Gospel account is true; however, some include certain events while leaving other events out. A chronological study integrates the four separate accounts narrated in the Gospels into a unified depiction of Jesus' ministry.

Specifically, for the discipleship pathway, we want to begin with the first three of the six significant stages of reference noted on the pathway. At these three stages, Jesus called his disciples with an invitation to 'come.'

These specific stages of reference are noted in the classic book, *Training of the Twelve* written by a Scottish churchman and theologian, Alexander Balmain Bruce in 1871. His book is a complete exposition of how Christ prepared his twelve disciples. In the 400 page book, Bruce says, "The twelve arrived at their final intimate relation to Jesus only by degrees, three stages in the history of their fellowship with Him being distinguishable." [1]

Come and See, Come and Follow, Come Be With Me

The three stages pointed out by Bruce are 'come and see' in John 1:35-46, 'come follow me' in Mark 1:16-20, and 'come be with me' in Mark 3:13-14. Also, by adding other study tools from Bible scholars like A.T. Robertson in his book, *Harmony of the Gospels*, helps to create a chronological timeline. Additionally, *The MacArthur Study Bible* has an excellent Chronology of the New Testament in its Introduction to the Gospels. By applying the chronological timeline, we learn the passage in John occurred about four to five months after Jesus was baptized and tempted in the wilderness. The Mark 1 passage is approximately ten to eleven months into Jesus' three-year ministry. In Mark 3, nearly two years into his ministry, 20 months to be more exact...Jesus chose the twelve disciples after a long night of prayer.

On the Relevant Discipleship Pathway™ the 'come and see' is outside the outer circle (stage 1). This part of the pathway depicts curiosity. In John 1:35-46, two disciples of John the Baptist, wanted to know where Jesus was staying. In verse 39, Jesus said, "Come, and you will see;" and the two men ended up spending the day with him.

After a season of curiosity, approximately ten to eleven months into Jesus' ministry, we read in Mark 1, where Andrew and his brother Simon Peter were casting their nets in the Sea of Galilee when Jesus said, "Come follow me." Although they were fishermen by trade, they left their nets and answered the call to follow him. It is within the outer concentric circle on the graphic where we practice the 7 Disciplines (stage 2). Today, as disciples, daily practicing the 7 Disciplines depicts our commitment to follow Christ. Remember, practicing a discipline a certain way is not about doing the discipline so we can check it off; rather, it's about practicing the discipline in order to make room to know and experience God.

> *Discipleship is a consciously chosen course of action producing transformation. Practicing the 7 Disciplines of a disciple makes room to experience God. @nelsonroth*

Twenty months after the start of Jesus' ministry, in Mark 3, Jesus spent the night in prayer to determine who out of all the disciples he would select to 'be with him.' The next morning, Jesus names the twelve disciples. The "be with him" depicts the importance of gathering as a group, as Jesus did with his disciples (stage 3). The 3Rs, in the middle of the concentric circles on the Relevant Discipleship Pathway™, are a picture of community and how small groups can function when they gather together.

The 3Rs represent the way Jesus and his disciples experienced community together. The first 'R' is being in relationship with God and others. Interrelationships or relating to others is a significant purpose for a small group when they gather. It is also important for small groups to scatter by getting outside of themselves. When we serve others, we experience the next 'R,' responding to what God is doing. That might be displayed in the midst of a group gathering or as a small group becomes a picture of Christ...one who served instead of being served and reaching out to others. A third core element of a healthy small group is revealing Christ, the final 'R' where individuals and the corporate group are living an incarnational life, which allows their lights to shine revealing Christ.

Overcoming Hesitations and What to Do

At this point, I'd like to interject a thought. Over the past several years, we have noticed two primary reasons why believers hesitate when it comes to investing their time in discipleship. From conversations we have had with believers, it seems most do not feel confident in 'what to do' and 'what to say.' We will address 'what to say' in the next chapter; but for now, let's consider 'what to do.' With what you have read so far, how might the Relevant Discipleship Pathway™ help you with 'what to do?' *Get into small groups or relationship with people*

So far, with the help of A.B. Bruce, we have a pathway with three stages. We have the 7 Disciplines and the 3Rs. Next on the pathway, we continue to get help with 'what to do.' As we've developed the discipleship coaching process we've discovered the journey along the pathway is not only inward, but also outward. The Relevant Discipleship Pathway™ goes beyond the first three stages to address three additional stages.

As we continue along the pathway, let's look at the fourth stage. Jesus gave final instructions to his disciples before he went to the cross. In John 15, Jesus said, "Abide in me and I in you." Referring back to the graphic in the Appendix on page 176, we are in the innermost circle; experiencing God. It is important to note that abiding in Christ and 'experiencing God' not only happens when we're gathered corporately as the church; but, also during personal times of solitude.

Change happens when we are in the presence of God. How have you experienced God's existence either in times gathering together with believers or in your time of personal solitude? Like the three disciples on top of the mountain at the time of the Transfiguration of Christ, we too might find ourselves wanting to stay in this incredible place. Let us encourage you to take the time you need to abide in Christ, to fully experience God and then to move out, and minister to others as the Spirit of God leads you.

Pause and Ponder

What have been your 'hesitations' for not engaging in discipleship?
As you begin to wrap your mind around the two graphics, how does it help with 'what to do'?

On the journey outward, we notice transformation happens at stage five on the pathway. Transformation in our lives is experienced around the 3Rs...through a relationship with God, responding to others and revealing Christ. Two years into his ministry, Jesus is preaching the Sermon on the Mount in Luke 6:40 when he says, "...everyone who is fully trained will be like their teacher." Then the sixth stage on the pathway, outside of all three circles, is about engaging culture and letting our light shine. Again, during the Sermon on the Mount in Matthew 5:14-16, Christ said, "...let your light shine before others."

A Way of Life for the Rest of Your Life

Once we've experienced the pathway, what's next? We're to continue, because the discipleship pathway is a continual process, a way of life. By comparing the continual process of the discipleship pathway as a place where we regularly walk on the carpet in our home, we would get an idea of how we're doing on the pathway by 'how worn the carpet is.'

Also, imagine the pathway can be non-linear as well as linear. This means as we continue to mature and grow as believers we could be at various points on the pathway at different times or even at several places at the same time. So the pathway isn't a rigid line to walk. Instead, like a dance, there is fluidity with specific realities to be regularly incorporated into your life.

Pause and Ponder

How is the system or framework of the Relevant Discipleship Pathway™ resonating with you? How would this pathway make a difference for you as a Christ follower?

Practicing the 7 Disciplines

Another vital part, for 'what to do,' is the 7 Disciplines we practice. We will learn what they are later in chapter five. For now, let me say this about the 7 Disciplines ... we find them in the DNA of the early church in Acts 2. The rationale for the seven specific disciplines is they also connect with the seven churches of Revelation.

Primarily the disciplines depict weaknesses pointed out by Jesus in the Revelation churches. While those seven churches were literal, first-century churches, they also are a picture of what churches will be like in the last days.

So, how close are we to Jesus coming again? Would a good, next question be, how is my church doing? Or an even better question might be, how am I doing because I am the church? What would it be like if all believers in a church would discipline themselves functioning as the first-century church? How might we experience such revitalization that we might know revival in our day?

> *Relevant Discipleship is less about a training program and more about how to become like Jesus. @nelsonroth*

In the matter of discipleship, not only 'what to do' but 'what to say' is a major hesitation. How would you benefit by overcoming 'what to say' if it is currently keeping you from moving forward as you'd like as a disciple of Christ? Let's see what we can discover about 'what to say' and the coaching approach to discipleship in the next chapter.

what leaders are saying...

My family and I have been serving God almost ten years as I have served being a pastor. But this year, I want to share about Relevant Discipleship and about the 7 disciplines. From the time I started discipleship one-to-one with my brother, Jesse McBride, many things started to change in my life I became more devoted to the Word of God especially in obedience. Through using what God has shown me, our church is learning a different focus on following Christ. Thank you firstly to God, secondly to this precious study of discipleship.

—Ramon Hernan Castellanos, Pastor
San Felipe Church
San Felipe, Orange Walk, Belize

The one-to-one disciple-making process utilizing the Relevant Discipleship Pathway was the missing ingredient and the perfect complement to the group discipleship opportunities already taking place in the faith community I serve. Our intentional discipleship process has truly been transformed through the use of the coaching approach to discipleship along with the support that we have received from Nelson and Pam... and yours can too.

—Rev. Wayne H. Clemens
Centerpoint Christian Fellowship Church
Barneveld, NY

The Relevant Discipleship Pathway gave me the tools for deeper conversations and the experience of coaching others. As a coach, I was already familiar with the techniques of deep listening, powerful questions, and action and accountability. However, I had been using those tools primarily for programs, not for strengthening a person's relationship to God. The coach approach helped me focus on my own discipleship, listen to others discipleship journeys, and practice asking those powerful questions that move people to action. As a result, I became more confident in sharing my discipleship experience with others and inviting them to join me in a group or in a one-to-one relationship that focuses on growing closer to God.

—Rev. Marilyn Wadkins
T.E.A.M. Ministries
Houston, TX

3 what to say

My wife, Pam, and I were leading a Train the Discipler™ Workshop at a church, and we started out by asking, "What really is holding you back from implementing discipleship?" A familiar response came back. One person said, "I know I should be discipling someone; but, I don't feel confident about what to say." Another said, "I don't feel like I know enough. What if someone asks a biblical question and I don't know the answer?"

I understand. I've been there. And, you probably have been there too. If so, read on because you may be surprised, as this group was, with Pam's answer. Pam said, "With the coaching approach you will be learning today, you will discover you ask questions; powerful questions that bring about discovery for the person you are discipling. The good news is you're not required to have all of the answers for the person you are discipling." With that information, the group became energized about the coaching approach to discipleship and became freed up that day from what was holding them back! How might this help you implement discipleship if you knew you didn't have to have all the answers?

> *Relevant Discipleship takes a coaching approach that helps the person you are discipling grow in their spiritual life and relationship with God. @nelsonroth*

Discipleship Coaching

If knowing 'what to say' is one of the biggest hesitations to discipleship, how might a coaching approach empower you as a disciple maker? As you've already read, you do not need all of the answers. With a coaching approach to discipleship, you can relax and enjoy incredible spiritual conversations with others. For you, as a disciple maker, praying and allowing the Holy Spirit to work is one of the most significant ways you can show up for a discipleship

> *If I mentor you, the tendency is for you to become like me. Relevant Discipleship takes a coaching approach where we both become more like Christ. @nelsonroth*

session. Then, as you listen intently, your powerful questions will be God-directed; instead of being directed by you.

I'm continually amazed how repeatedly people come up with creative solutions and plans when the coaching approach is used in the discipleship session.

The coaching approach allows the person being discipled an opportunity to express what they have been thinking, and to be validated in the process. Through the process, the person being discipled takes ownership of the plan because it fits best at that time with their situation and style. Otherwise, without a coaching approach, the tendency might be to prescribe or impose a particular solution that we may think would work best. Unfortunately, nearly without fail, this is not the best approach.

Pause and Ponder

How empowering does a coaching approach seem to you?
What happens to you when you make a discovery?
How motivated are you to follow through when something is your idea?
How does the accountability level increase when a personal commitment is made to a plan?

Pam and I live in South Mississippi on the Gulf Coast, between Mobile and New Orleans. When it comes to being able to eat fantastic food, you will find it on the Gulf Coast; whether it's at a fine dining restaurant or a gas station. The reason the food is so fantastic is what the cooks or chefs may call their 'secret sauce;' which kicks up the taste a notch. I like to think that coaching is the 'secret sauce' to Relevant Discipleship™. Let's consider why coaching takes discipleship up a notch.

Three Coaching Techniques

Coaching seems to be a 'buzzword' right now, and it's possible for a person to call themselves a coach; and yet, not be proficient in using trained coaching competencies. The purpose of this chapter is to provide you with three coaching techniques incorporated in the Nehemiah Response Coaching Model™; not to train you to be a professional coach, but to equip you as disciple maker. Disciple makers utilizing the coaching approach ask powerful questions rather than tell, are good listeners, and provide accountability to the person while they are making discovery and creating actions steps. These coaching techniques, when applied with the discipleship pathway, result in meaningful and transformational changes in a person's life.

Powerful Questions

Let's consider Jesus and his discipleship style. Jesus had spiritual conversations using coaching skills long before the term coaching was recognized. He asked a lot of questions. In fact, Jesus asked over three hundred questions which are recorded in the New Testament. Jesus shifted from being a teller like the Pharisees to asking compelling questions that caused a person to stop and really think about their life. Take a look at the list of some questions

More than 300 times in the Gospels, Jesus asked questions! @nelsonroth

gathered from the Scriptures. Which questions impact you?

- What do you want? (John 1:38)
- How many loaves do you have? (Matthew 15:34)
- Who do you say that I am? (Matthew 16:15)
- What good will it be for someone to gain the whole world, yet forfeit their soul? (Matthew 16:26)
- What do you want me to do for you? (Matthew 20:32)

In Matthew 16, we see Jesus asking his disciples, "Who do people say the Son of Man is?" His disciples answered with some of the comments they heard from the crowds and then, Jesus said to the disciples, "But who do you say I am?" (Matthew 16:15).

Can you see those men thinking long and hard to have the right answer? Why do you think Jesus asked the disciples a question instead of telling them who he was? Jesus could have just told them like many of us do, but he refrained. Jesus waited patiently for the disciples to make the discovery. Let's look in on the conversation between Peter and Jesus recorded in Matthew 16:16-17. "Simon Peter answered, 'You are the Messiah, the Son of the living God.' Jesus replied, 'Blessed are you, Simon son of Jonah, for this was not revealed to you by flesh and blood, but by my Father in heaven.'" So, what might have been the outcome for Peter when he responded with the right answer?

Powerful questions like the questions Jesus asked his disciples are open-ended; leaving room for a person to respond with answers that could set them on course for a plan and purpose to grow spiritually. Most often, people ask closed-ended questions, only allowing for 'yes' or 'no' answers; or at best, a short statement. For example:

- Did your discipleship focus go well?
- Do you need more time to reach your goal?

What do you notice about the above questions? If you answered, "Both of the questions are closed-ended," you're getting the hang of asking powerful questions that are open-ended like the following examples.

- What did you discover during your discipleship focus?
- How would you assess where you are with your goal?

J. Val Hastings, the founder of Coaching4Clergy, says this about asking powerful questions in his book, *The Next Great Awakening*. "One of a coach's greatest tools is powerful questions. Powerful questions are usually open-ended, leaving room for contemplation and reflection, instead of being limited to yes or no or specific choices." [1]

Now that you have a better understanding of powerful questions, I would like to encourage you to practice, practice, practice asking powerful questions.

Change those closed-ended questions into open-ended questions by starting out with these two words...'what' and 'how.' Now, go for it! You're on your way to asking powerful questions; how are you doing with listening?

Deep Listening

Like Jesus, coaches ask powerful, thought-provoking questions. Then, out of a sense of confidence, are okay keeping quiet, listening deeply, and waiting for the person they are coaching to respond. This book is not to prepare you to be a professional coach; but, to equip you as a disciple maker with basic coaching techniques to develop a coaching approach to your spiritual conversations with others.

Of course, there were times when Jesus spoke directly to a situation, and good coaches know how and when to do that, too. Primarily, a coaching approach to discipleship is about the disciple maker being inquisitive. To be inquisitive, you need to be fully present and intently listen because listening is one of the greatest gifts we can give to someone. However, listening doesn't come naturally and takes practice. Often our normal response is to tell or to fix the situation. Coaching is usually 80% listening, with the other 20% being powerful questions and validating the person you are discipling; allowing space for the person to make their own discovery. Let's look at some ways to develop excellent listening skills.

- Being curious and interested

- Quieting our mind and being fully present
- Creating a safe space for the other person
- Exploring possibilities instead of giving answers
- Really getting the other person

Action and Accountability

The third of the three coaching techniques we teach at the discipleship coaching level is action and accountability. This particular technique is where the person you are discipling puts a plan together and commits to follow through. Action and accountability can include some of the following questions:

- What do you want to do?
- What has worked before?
- What do you know you can do?
- How is God speaking to you?
- What is a good first step?
- What is possible?
- What will you do?
- What would you like to say happened when we get together next time?

There is a graphic of the Nehemiah Response Coaching Model™ in the Appendix of this book on page 177. For a more thorough and comprehensive look at the coaching approach and the three techniques we share with you in this chapter, read *Nehemiah Response: a coaching model.* The Nehemiah Response Coaching Model™ is a biblical, transformational process for revitalization and change. The model captures responses of Nehemiah and will help you develop a custom solution to get from where you are (Present Situation) to where you want to go (Preferred Future). The Nehemiah Response Coaching Model™ provides a reproducible and repeatable strategic process for positive change in life and ministry. Coupled along with the Relevant Discipleship Pathway™, a disciple maker will have the tools necessary for 'what to do' and 'what to say' when it comes to discipleship.

> *Imagine, every believer empowered with a coaching approach to being and making disciples. @nelsonroth*

Whatever your current experience is around coaching, we hope this chapter has given insight to this leadership skill and will help you to begin to think about what a coaching approach to discipleship might look like for you. When the time is right for you for training in this area, Relevant Ministry, Inc. has several ongoing training opportunities for you to consider. Check out the information in the What's Next section on page 171 and on our website - www.relevantministry.org/training.

Pause and Ponder

What's your untapped potential?
How might a coaching approach be the missing ingredient for you when it comes to discipleship?

what leaders are saying...

Jesus never coerced, pushed, or forced anyone to follow him...he simply met people where they were, asked powerful questions and led by example. Changing the way we think about how to share the Gospel simply by employing coaching techniques opens up so many possibilities. Discipleship coaching releases the pastor or layperson from answering the questions to asking them... allowing those we lead to discover, experience and deepen their relationship with Jesus. By creating such a culture of coaching we can begin to see the Great Commission (Matthew 28:18-20) and the Greatest Commandment (Matthew 22:36-40) collide at the core of every believer causing a true revival in the church and in the world. As a pastor for more than 25 years, I am so excited about Relevant Discipleship and the coaching approach. It will serve me well in the remaining years of my professional ministry and my life as a Christ-follower.

—Rev. DeeDee Autry, PCC, Senior Pastor
Mountainside United Methodist Church
Hot Springs Village, AR

I just wanted to let you know how helpful the Relevant Discipleship Pathway and our one-to-one discipleship coaching sessions have been for my thinking and planning about discipleship in our church. I think of all the "tools" I've picked up since Seminary, coaching may actually be the most helpful practically speaking to what I'm trying to do in ministry, so thank you for giving a thorough introduction to the practice.

—Adam L. Brice, Pastor
Resurrection Presbyterian Church
West Lafayette, IN

While I have been deeply committed to the practice of discipleship throughout my ministry, I have also been frequently disappointed in the various methods and materials I've used. Discipleship Coaching has changed that! I have been able to immediately employ the content and methods learned through the Nehemiah Response Coaching Model in my individual discipleship coaching and with my church's disciple-making emphasis in our small group ministry. I am walking into the next ministry season invigorated and filled with anticipation of seeing disciples making disciples!

—Joe Donaldson
Associate Pastor and Discipleship Coach
Journey Church
Federal Way, WA

4 first things first

There is a story in the Bible of a 'rich' man who asked Jesus, "...what good thing must I do to get eternal life?" (Matthew 19:16). Some Bible teachers have called this person the possible thirteenth disciple, because of Jesus' invitation in verse 21, "Then come, follow me." After assuring himself he was keeping all the commandments; and yet, sensing he was still missing something, the rich man asked, "What do I still lack?" Jesus puts his finger on a sensitive spot, in verse 21, by saying, "...sell your possessions...Then come, follow me."

Undoubtedly, this young man had a lot of 'something' he preferred over Jesus. The term used in the Bible regarding the condition of this man was 'rich.' He was wealthy ... in other words, very rich and he had a lot of money; however, it could have been anything. Anything that gets in the way or 'something' we prefer and choose over Jesus will keep us from being fully committed to following him. Either way, whether money or things, as a result of the wrong choice, we see in

Matthew 19:22, the person "went away sad." Scripture makes it pretty clear...to be a disciple; one must choose Jesus over everything else.

Pause and Ponder

When did your journey with God begin?
What's your current relationship with God?

Knowing Christ

So, to be a disciple, to be a fully committed follower of Christ...it's first things first. Somewhere along the way on our life journey, a curiosity rises about life, death, and our future causing us to come to terms with our mortality. Like the rich, young ruler, we have a decision to make when we realize we can't change our past; but, we can determine our destiny by choosing Christ.

Like the disciples we read about in the New Testament, you may hang around in a religious setting or with spiritual people being curious for a while. You may even do some good deeds and follow the rules. You would not be the first person to do that. The Scriptures tell us that's what Peter did. As you think about your conversion story, let's consider what we know about Peter and when he might have been converted.

Salvation is knowing and following Jesus Christ. John 10:27-28, "My sheep listen to my voice; I know them and they follow me. I give them eternal life..." @nelsonroth

We know, early on, Peter dropped his fishing nets and began to walk with Jesus. We read in the Scriptures how he struggled, even up to the night of Christ's crucifixion when he denied he was with Jesus. We know Peter's eyes were opened in Matthew 16:16 when he said, "you are the Messiah, the Son of the living God." We also know after he denied Christ and went back to fishing, he later repented and returned. Jesus then reinstates Peter in John chapter twenty-one when he asks Peter three times, "Simon son of John, do you love me more than these?" Jesus was asking what Peter would choose. Like the rich young ruler, Peter was 'rich' when it came to fishing, but to what would he say yes? Somewhere along the way, Peter opened his heart and said 'yes' to Jesus.

Pause and Ponder

To what will you say yes?
What's your conversion story?

Christian or Disciple

Today, we call people Christians when they pray to receive Christ; but, I wonder if we are correctly using the term? In the Gospels, followers were called disciples. In fact, we see the word 'disciple' over 280 times and the word 'Christian' is not even in the Gospels. The word Christian is found the first time, of just three times, in Acts eleven where we read, "The disciples were called Christians first at Antioch." That's because people noticed the disciples Christ-likeness

> *The word Christian is used three times in the New Testament, and the word disciple is used over 280 times and clearly preferred by the NT writers. What's with that? @nelsonroth*

and called them, Christians.

What do you think? Is it appropriate to immediately call a person a Christian at their conversion? I'm not saying this person didn't have a salvation experience when he or she sincerely prayed to repent and receive Christ; nor, am I asserting you have to work for your salvation. However, I am suggesting as a person begins to move past the stage of curiosity and makes a choice about his or her conversion or salvation; he or she is a Christ follower and yet, he or she may not entirely resemble Christ.

So, first things first. The next step then is to be a disciple. Realizing your need for a Savior, repenting of sin, and receiving Christ into your life. Then continuing to follow, being transformed to be like Christ. And, at some point along your lifelong journey people will notice and call you Christian.

> As for you, you were dead in your transgressions and sins, in which you used to live when you followed the ways of this world and of the ruler of the kingdom of the air, the spirit who is now at work in those who are disobedient. All of us also

lived among them at one time, gratifying the cravings of our flesh and following its desires and thoughts. Like the rest, we were by nature deserving of wrath. But because of his great love for us, God, who is rich in mercy, made us alive with Christ even when we were dead in transgressions—it is by grace you have been saved. And God raised us up with Christ and seated us with him in the heavenly realms in Christ Jesus, in order that in the coming ages he might show the incomparable riches of his grace, expressed in his kindness to us in Christ Jesus. For it is by grace you have been saved, through faith—and this is not from yourselves, it is the gift of God—not by works, so that no one can boast. For we are God's handiwork, created in Christ Jesus to do good works, which God prepared in advance for us to do. (Ephesians 2:1-10)

Pause and Ponder

What is a person's condition before they know God? How would you describe your relationship with God? What does the offer of grace mean to you?

In this matter of grace and discipleship, Dietrich Bonhoeffer in *The Cost of Discipleship*, calls conversion without discipleship, 'cheap grace.' The term, 'cheap grace' is something to ponder as we start the journey of following Christ. Grace is costly from God's perspective because he offered up his only Son. It can be cheap, as Bonhoeffer notes, because of our response to God's grace.

> Cheap grace is the preaching of forgiveness without requiring repentance, baptism without church discipline, communion without confession, absolution without personal confession. Cheap grace is grace without discipleship, grace without the cross, grace without Jesus Christ, living and incarnate. [1]

Pause and Ponder

What's your relationship with God?
What are your thoughts about 'cheap grace?'
How has 'cheap grace' minimized the need for or importance of discipleship in the Church today?

The Most Important Relationship

Let's take the next few minutes to explore further the most important relationship of all. The purpose of the following paragraphs is first, to better understand God's plan of redeeming humanity and realizing my personal need if I am without Christ. And secondly, to more greatly appreciate God's love if I am a believer and have experienced redemption or salvation.

The word 'redeem' means to buy back, to repurchase, and to be free from the bondage of sin. The word 'salvation' is a big or prominent word. Prominent in the sense that it covers the meaning of many other words like redemption, delivered, forgiven, pardoned, restored, and others.

The word salvation suggests there are those who need to be saved. The Bible leaves no doubt as to who they are, Romans 3:23, "...for all have sinned and fall short of the glory of God." In 1 Timothy 1:15, the Apostle Paul includes himself saying, "Christ Jesus came into the world to save sinners—of whom I am the worst."

The term salvation is commonly used to describe the act by which a person is delivered from a threatening condition that puts the person in danger. For example, we say a person was saved or rescued from drowning, from a burning building, or a sinking ship. In each of these cases three things had to happen:

- The person saved was in danger.
- Someone saw his danger and went to his rescue.
- The rescuer was successful and the person was delivered from his or her perilous plight.

Since the fall of humankind recorded in Genesis chapter three, when Adam and Eve yielded to Satan's temptation and broke God's commandment, every human being has been under God's condemnation, Romans 5:12-21. In verse 12 we read, "Therefore, just as sin entered the world through one man, and death through sin, and in this way death came to all people, because all sinned." However, the good news found in the same passage in verses 18 and 19 reads, "Consequently, just as one trespass resulted in condemnation for all people, so also one righteous act resulted in justification and life for all people. For just as through the disobedience of the one man the many were made sinners, so also through the obedience of the one man the many will be made righteous."

Paul is explaining how everyone is a sinner and how it is that Christ's death can give an ungodly sinner a right standing before God. 1 Corinthians 15:22 says, "For as in Adam all die, so in Christ all will be made alive."

Sin means to miss the mark; which includes both our attitude and action. Sin also means to overstep the forbidden line; this consists of both our inability to do right and the inclination to do wrong.

In physical birth, all humans are from the loins of Adam. We identify with him. Adam's original sin is our sin. Romans 3:10 says, "As it is written: 'There is no one righteous, not even one.'" Psalms 51:5 reads, "Surely I was sinful at birth, sinful from the time my mother conceived me."

Salvation, first of all, is necessary because of the sin. Secondly, salvation or redemption is required because of the righteousness of God. God is a Holy God and must punish sin. Let's look at John 8:21-24. Verse 24 reads, "I told you that you would die in your sins; if you do not believe that I am he, you will indeed die in your sins." Revelation 20:15 says, "Anyone whose name was not found written in the book of life was thrown into the lake of fire."

God is a Holy God and must punish sin; God is also a God of love and has provided the way of salvation. This salvation is the good news of the Gospel! Read Romans 5:6-9. Verse 6 says, "You see, at just the right time, when we were still powerless, Christ died for the ungodly." John 3:16 says, "For God so loved the world that he gave his one and only Son, that whoever believes in him shall not perish but have eternal life." 1 John 3:16 reads, "This is how we know what love is: Jesus Christ laid down his life for us."

God loves the whole world! Who then, will have eternal life? John, says in verse 3:16, "...whoever believes in him shall not perish." As individuals, we each determine our destiny by choosing or not choosing Christ!

To continue the familiar John 3:16 passage, verses 17 and 18 proclaim, "For God did not send his Son into the world to condemn the world, but to save the world through him. Whoever believes in him is not condemned, but whoever does not believe stands condemned already because they have not believed in the name of God's one and only Son."

How is salvation initiated? What action does an individual need to take? In Acts 16:30, the jailer asked, "...what must I do to be saved?" In verse 31, Paul and Silas replied, "Believe in the Lord Jesus, and you will be saved." In Acts 16:29, the jailor "...fell trembling." A person must know their need first, and their inability to save themselves as seen in the jailor's initial response.

cts 20:21 makes it clear that believing in Jesus ˥an head knowledge and requires repentance. ...ᵥ ᵥᵉⁱˢᵉ states, "I have declared to both Jews and Greeks that they must turn to God in repentance and have faith in our Lord Jesus." Repentance is admitting your spiritual need. It means to make a 180-degree turn. Repentance means a genuine sorrow toward God on account of our sin. Repentance involves the humble act of self-surrender to the will of God. To believe is to acknowledge that Christ died for you.

Pause and Ponder

How can this happen for me if I have not yet repented and received Christ?
What must I do to have eternal life?
What is keeping me from making this important decision about my destiny?

Romans 6:23, "For the wages of sin is death, but the gift of God is eternal life in Christ Jesus our Lord." To believe in Jesus Christ is to possess eternal life, and to have "...crossed over from death to life" (John 5:24).

Pause and Ponder

Are you in a personal relationship with God?
Do you know him in your head and your heart?

In 2 Timothy 1:12, Paul said he didn't just know about God, but genuinely "...I know whom I have believed, and am convinced that he is able to guard what I have entrusted in him until that day." Paul was in relationship with God because there was a time in his life when he realized he needed the salvation God had to offer. In Acts 9, we learn about the time Paul opened his heart and turned to God, receiving the redemption God had to offer through Jesus Christ. When Paul acknowledged his need and turned to God, he was made alive in Christ. When were you made alive in Christ?

Jesus began his earthly ministry with this message in Matthew 4:17, "Repent, for the kingdom of heaven has come near." Today, he is still giving the same invitation to come. The kingdom is near, or is available. It's now your choice.

The following words written in 1874 describe the possible timeline of a not-yet believer to become a committed follower of Christ. These are words credited to Theodore Monod, written during a series of consecration meetings in Broadlands, England. How do the words of this poem, *None of Self and All of Thee*, speak to you?

None of Self and All of Thee [2]

O the bitter shame and sorrow,
That a time could ever be,
When I proudly said to Jesus,
All of self, and none of Thee!

Yet He found me, and I beheld Him
Bleeding on the cruel tree,

And my wistful heart said faintly,
Some of self, and some of Thee!

Day by day His tender mercy,
Healing, helping, full and free,
Brought me lower, while I whispered,
Less of self, and more of Thee!

Higher than the highest heavens,
Deeper than the deepest sea, Lord,
Thy love at last hath conquered:
None of self, and all of Thee!

what leaders are saying...

Even though I have been a Christian for 35 years, I believe the Relevant Discipleship Pathway challenged me to take my spiritual journey to another level. I would recommend strongly discipleship coaching to all believers as we work toward achieving the Great Commission.
—Tom Granoff, Ph.D., PCC
Dissertation Statistician/Methodologist/
Professor
Pepperdine University
Malibu, CA

I have experienced a wonderful new opportunity to learn and grow in my own walk with Christ as well as to share His love through the Relevant Discipleship Pathway. I greatly appreciated the theology of the pathway and discipleship coaching, as it is extremely balanced.

—Dr. David P. Hyatt, PCC
Effective Ministries Coaching and Consulting
St. Louis, MO

Nelson and Pam have a passion to see disciples of Jesus make disciples of Jesus for the glory of God. They've committed their lives to this endeavor, and have developed a practical way to help others understand and live discipleship as "a way of life for the rest of your life" in complete dependence upon the Holy Spirit. Every time Nelson and I engaged in the Relevant Discipleship Pathway together, I was greatly encouraged and sharpened in my own relationship with Jesus and eager to coach others in a disciple-making way of life. You hold helpful and encouraging material in your hands!

—Erik Johnson
Pastor of Worship and Disciplemaking
Crosspoint Community Church
Eureka, IL

5 practicing the 7 disciplines

What does it mean to you to be intentional? The dictionary uses the word deliberate. In other words, not accidental. So, as we live the life of a disciple, we're to be deliberate about our practice of the disciplines in order to experience God at work and then to join him in that work.

Intentionality

This past spring, I was busy with other things, and I neglected the flower beds in our front yard. The perennials came up nice; unfortunately, so did the weeds. Left alone the weeds soon took over. Like the perennials, in our spiritual life there are natural organic processes; that's God's part. Our part is to partner with him in the process.

Scripture is clear we don't work for our salvation, it's a gift given by grace. Ephesians 2:8-9 reads, "For it is by grace you have been saved, through faith—and this is not from yourselves, it is the gift of God—not by works, so that no one can boast." Then in verse ten we see our part, "For we are God's handiwork, created in Christ Jesus to do good works, which God prepared in advance for us to do." Let's call it responsibility and our part to intentionally grow and mature as a believer.

> Discipleship is personal development that requires self-denial. What does your journey of following look like? @nelsonroth

As we experience the Relevant Discipleship Pathway™, we refer to our part as practicing the 7 Disciplines. By practicing the disciplines, we give validity to Paul's words to the Philippian church. In Philippians 2:12-13, Paul encourages fellow believers, "Therefore, my dear friends, as you have always obeyed —not only in my presence, but now much more in my absence—continue to work out your salvation with fear and trembling, for it is God who works in you to will and to act in order to fulfill his good purpose."

The 7 Disciplines

So, what do we do? What are the disciplines to practice? Let's go to the early church to find out. We learn from the time the early believers came together as the church; they operated around several spiritual disciplines found in Acts 2:42-47. These disciplines were a part of their DNA. Take a few minutes and in your Bible, read these verses in Acts two, then we'll identify and give short descriptions of the 7 Disciplines a follower of Christ practices on the Relevant Discipleship Pathway™.

Let's identify each of the 7 Disciplines and give a short description for each one. First, in Acts 2:42, four of the 7 Disciplines are found:

"They devoted themselves..." or they were fully committed. To be a devoted follower is the discipline of (1) **Discipleship**. The discipline of Discipleship is an excellent place to begin with since everything we are talking about is discipleship. As a discipline, Discipleship is about 'being' rather than 'doing.' It's about character and 'who' you are.

> **Discipleship** is growing godly in character with a foundation of personal values and purpose.

"They devoted themselves **to the apostles' teaching...**" or the (2) **Word**.

The **Word** is developing a deep relationship with God and having a passion for knowing him more.

"They devoted themselves...**to fellowship**" or (3) **Community**.

> **Community** is loving one another and sharing life.

"They devoted themselves...**to the breaking of bread and to prayer**" or the discipline of (4) **Prayer**.

> **Prayer** is communicating with God alone and with others.

Next in Acts 2:45, we see the early church sacrificed to be generous and "...**to give to anyone who had need**" or the discipline of (5) **Ministry**. Serving like Jesus who "...did not come to be served, but to serve" Matthew 20:28.

> **Ministry** is discovering spiritual gifts and serving like Christ.

In Acts 2:47, they are "...**praising God**" which is the discipline of (6) **Worship**.

> **Worship** is experiencing God when gathered with other believers and through the week as a lifestyle.

The outcome of the practice of the disciplines was people in the city of Jerusalem, not-yet believers, committing their lives to Christ. This is the discipline of (7) **Evangelism**; also found in Acts 2:47, "**...enjoying the favor of all the people. And the Lord added to their number daily those who were being saved.**"

> **Evangelism** is cultivating intentional friendships with not-yet believers.

The 7 Disciplines of a disciple depicted on the Relevant Discipleship Pathway™ graphic, found in the Appendix on page 176, flow inward, making room to experience God. Remember the practice of the discipline is not about checking it off of a list and saying, "I did it today." Rather, asking the question, "Did my practice 'make room' for me to experience God?" Then, there's an outward flow from the center bringing transformation in our lives around the 3Rs. We will learn more about the 3Rs and transformation in the next chapter; but first, let's look at an insightful quote from Richard Foster about how practicing the disciplines is 'a way of sowing to the Spirit'.

> A farmer is helpless to grow grain; all he can do is provide the right conditions for the growing of grain. He cultivates the ground, he plants the seed, he waters the plants, and then the natural forces of the

earth take over and up comes the grain. ...This is the way it is with the Spiritual Disciplines - they are a way of sowing to the Spirit. ...By themselves the Spiritual Disciplines can do nothing; they can only get us to the place where something can be done. [1]

The Church in the Last Days

In chapter two, we mentioned the rationale for the 7 Disciplines we are practicing not only come from the DNA of the New Testament church; but also, from the seven churches of Revelation! Let's focus in on those seven churches.

The New Testament book of Revelation unpacks all things future beginning in chapter four. There are various views on how those events unfold. For now, what we do know is that Jesus is coming again, and soon. In Revelation 1:19, we have an outline for the entire book of Revelation. Jesus said to John who was on the Island of Patmos, "Write, therefore, what you have seen, what is now and what will take place later." Revelation chapter one is about the past, 'what you have seen.' Chapter two and three are about the present, 'what is now.' And chapters four to twenty-two 'what will take place later' with the last words of Jesus in the Bible being, "Yes, I am coming soon" (Revelation 22:20).

So, as we consider chapters two and three, the present things; we discover seven letters written to particular churches in the province of Asia of that time. These were literal churches, and already each church had deficiencies revealed by Christ's examination in these chapters. Today, we can also learn from this examination because these seven churches are also types of what churches will be like in the last days, before the coming of Christ.

We can look at each church and ask, "How is the church doing?" Or, "As I consider what Christ's examination of a certain church reveals, upon an honest assessment, what might I need to rename my church?"

As mentioned before, an even better question might be, "Since I am the church, how am I doing?" Each of the 7 Disciplines we've identified in the DNA of the early church in Acts connects with the seven churches of Revelation by either what Christ commended or warned about as he evaluated those churches. Knowing the DNA of the early church and the connection with the churches in Revelation is an incredible rationale for the 7 Disciplines of a disciple of the Relevant Discipleship Pathway™.

Let's take a brief look at each of the seven churches and the discipline that it represents for us on the pathway of discipleship.

Ephesus had "...forsaken the love you had at first." Revelation 2:4
The discipline of **Worship.**

To **Smyrna**, Jesus said pray and without saying it suggests warfare prayer, "Do not be afraid...the devil will put some of you in prison to test you...Be faithful..." Revelation 2:10
The discipline of **Prayer**.

Pergamos held "...to the teaching of the Nicolaitans. Repent therefore!" Revelation 2:15-16
The discipline of the **Word**.

Thyatira loved the world and was only concerned about self. "You tolerate that woman Jezebel...By her teaching she misleads my servants." Revelation 2:20
The discipline of **Ministry**.

Sardis had fallen asleep and was just going through the motions. "Wake up!" Revelation 3:2
The discipline of **Discipleship**.

Philadelphia, 'philea' means brotherly love. "I have placed before you an open door..." Revelation 3:8
The discipline of **Community**.

Laodecia was self-sufficient and inward focused. "...you are lukewarm..." Revelation 3:16
The discipline of **Evangelism**.

How to Practice the 7 Disciplines

We now have something to be intentional about; and, it's not a super long list. It's a total of 7 Disciplines of a disciple; the practice of which seems doable. We realize there are other vital spiritual actions of a believer like generosity, simplicity, journaling, fasting, and the list could go on and on. These are all good; however, making a long list of disciplines can be overwhelming. Through several years of working with disciples, we've discovered all other spiritual actions are particular ways to 'practice' the 7 Disciplines while journeying on the Relevant Discipleship Pathway™. So, when you feel the Lord leading, go ahead and journal or fast. For example, journaling is a great way to practice the discipline of the Word; and, fasting is a way you can practice the discipline of Prayer from time to time.

> *Relevant Discipleship leaves the classroom and, through relationships and practical application, Christ is revealed in your life. @nelsonroth*

When you begin the Relevant Discipleship Pathway™ or if you are already on the journey of being a disciple of Christ, which one of the 7 Disciplines will you focus on next? And, how is the Lord leading you to practice this discipline at the present time on the Relevant Discipleship Pathway™? During each discipline's focus between your discipleship coaching sessions, the *Relevant Discipleship™ Resource Manual* is a great reference with articles, coaching tools, and lessons.

Choosing a discipline to focus on brings us to another significant concept around the 7 Disciplines. There isn't a particular order to practice the 7 Disciplines. You will experience growth as you focus on the discipline most relevant to you at the time. Your focus is about what God wants to reveal to you. During a particular discipline focus, the others aren't to be neglected because a healthy balance of each discipline is vital as you grow and mature.

How did Jesus teach his disciples? When the disciples asked Jesus about 'how to pray,' did he say, "That's in chapter eight, and we'll get there in three weeks?" No, he stopped right there and then and shared about the discipline of Prayer.

Along with the Relevant Discipleship Pathway™, we've found that the coaching approach, we shared in Chapter 3, to be a perfect way to bring about discovery in the discipleship process. The coach or the discipler doesn't direct the disciplee; instead, they listen and ask powerful questions. Coaching contextualizes discipleship and considers where the disciplee is at the time! The coaching approach to discipleship helps to keep us from telling or prescribing what the person being discipled needs to do next.

Forming New Habits

When we practice the 7 Disciplines, we form new habits. Did you know that as believers we still struggle with the flesh? In Romans 7:18-20, Paul says, "For I know that good itself does not dwell in me, that is, in my sinful nature. For I have the desire to do what is good, but I cannot carry it out. For I do not do the good I want to do, but the evil I do not want to do— this I keep on doing. Now if I do what I do not want to do, it is no longer I who do it, but it is sin living in me that does it."

Pause and Ponder

What would be an important next step for you on this discipleship journey?
When you practice the 7 Disciplines, what do you think might begin to happen?

Pam recently purchased a new set of flatware. It came with a tray to slip into a cabinet drawer. When she replaced the previous set of flatware, she discovered the new tray was deeper than the cabinet drawer. She solved the problem by moving the flatware to another, deeper drawer in a cabinet a few feet away. Dish towels were in that drawer, so she switched them over to the other drawer. Problem solved! But, instead, it created another situation for me. You see, I am a creature of habit. I get up early every morning and make coffee; I routinely get a spoon to measure the amount I want to make. So, you guessed it. The first day, I opened the drawer where the flatware had always been, only to find dish towels. I quickly noticed I had a habit I needed to break. Moving forward, I confess I opened the wrong drawer for nine days. Gradually, with intentionality, I broke the old habit and created a new one.

About creating new habits when we are practicing the disciplines, Richard Foster gives this important warning about the possibility of the disciplines becoming legalistic and misfiring.

> How can we be shaped in such a way that our life becomes an expression of the spirit of Christ himself? ...Many spiritual practices support this process: public and private worship, study, prayer, reading and memorizing Scripture, reflecting on God's activity in nature and history, and service to others. Other spiritual disciplines such as the practices of solitude, silence and fasting also facilitate spiritual formation. But these activities can also misfire and become burdensome, killing the very life we seek. All spiritual disciplines require care to produce growth and progress. [2]

Just like I learned a new habit by consciously practicing which drawer was the right drawer to retrieve a spoon; when we practice the 7 Disciplines, we end up forming new habits in our life as believers and followers of Jesus Christ. Ultimately, we overcome in our struggle with the flesh and become more transformed like him. Transformation, through cooperating with the Holy Spirit, is the supreme outcome.

> The *Relevant Discipleship coaching approach to discipleship provides the support most people need to form new habits to get traction and move forward.* @nelsonroth

Outcomes of the Relevant Discipleship Pathway™ and transformation will be our specific focus in the next chapter. However, for right now, how is God speaking to you about intentionality?

what leaders are saying...

The Relevant Discipleship Pathway has become a lifesaver for me. My frustration has been with programs and classes that produce smarter Christians; yet, not necessarily mature believers. I'm excited to discover how this process will be planted within my local church.
> — Bil Barkley, LPC
> Minister of Education and Senior Adults
> First Baptist Church
> Mount Pleasant, TX

The Relevant Discipleship process has changed the way I walk with Jesus. Reading the Word was just a "yes, I did it" moment; but, now it is my daily food. I can't do anything without looking at my guide the "Word." When Nelson and I were on the discipline of the Word it made me understand that when you know and experience the author, you love and appreciate the reading more. The Relevant Discipleship one-to-one sessions helped me to have an accountable person. To know that there is someone, I'm in relationship with, and to talk about God with is very encouraging. I'm excited about what is happening in my church around discipleship. I can imagine all of our Garifuna churches implementing Relevant Discipleship.

—Pedro Castro, Discipleship Overseer
Evangelical Garifuna Church
New Orleans, LA

Walking an intentional, inquisitive journey of discovery into a new reality of Christ. This describes the transforming experience I discovered with Relevant Discipleship.

—Rev. Lilian Reyneke
Methodist Church of South Africa
Orkney Society South Africa

I have had the privilege of being coached through Relevant Discipleship by Nelson Roth. As we have worked through the seven disciplines, I have never failed to experience both insight and steps of positive growth. This was particularly true in the disciplines of prayer and ministry. Both of these areas of my spiritual life have been strengthened because of the time spent with Nelson. I would recommend Relevant Discipleship to anyone who is looking to grow both their personal walk with Jesus and as a tool for them to impact the spiritual lives of others.

—Len Thebarge, Senior Associate Pastor
Grace Church
Normal, IL

6 the outcome, ongoing transformation

The Apostle Paul challenged Timothy in his discipleship when he said, "...train yourself to be godly" in 1 Timothy 4:7. Disciples discipline themselves for their personal spiritual development. We talked about the importance of intentionality in the last chapter. By being intentional about the discipleship journey, practicing the 7 Disciplines, and by yielding to the indwelling of the Holy Spirit, we become more like Christ.

Transformed Around the 3Rs

The outcome of practicing the 7 Disciplines is godliness. When we do what we can do, God will do what only he can do! This statement reminds me of the principle out of the story of the raising of Lazarus. In John chapter eleven, Jesus came to the tomb and said to the crowd, "Take away the stone." When those who were gathered around Lazarus' tomb hesitated and questioned Jesus, he responded, "Did I not tell you that if you believe, you would see the glory of God?" In

John 11:41, they took action and did what they could do. "So they took away the stone." Then, Jesus did what only he could do. "Jesus called in a loud voice, 'Lazarus, come out!' The deadman came out..." Lazarus arose from the grave.

As we 'train ourselves for godliness,' we're doing our part in the discipleship process. God, in turn, does what only he can do. Likewise, there will be miraculous, transformational outcomes as you practice the 7 Disciplines.

> *The disciplines become evidence of spiritual health in life and ministry. They make room for Christ to work from the inside out.*
> *@nelsonroth*

On the Relevant Discipleship Pathway™, there is transformation and it's around the 3Rs; the core of the three concentric circles graphic. See the 3Rs in the Appendix on page 176. As you're on the pathway, you'll experience...

- Relationships with God and others
- Responding to how God is at work
- The discovery of opportunities to Reveal Christ in your life!

The 3Rs come directly from the Greatest Commandment and the Great Commission of the New Testament. These core values are vital in your discipleship process and are evidences of spiritual health in life and ministry.

Pause and Ponder

How are you currently seeing God at work in your life in these three areas?
What might be the things that will hold you back from being transformed?
What is the stone only you can roll away?

Our Responsibility

What would have happened if those gathered at Lazarus' tomb that day chose not to listen and obey Jesus? How might this story of Lazarus play out differently if the disobedience of bystanders kept Jesus from doing his part? It certainly is something to consider. In what way might you be keeping God from working the way only he can in your life?

Consider the words to the song "Day by Day" from the musical Godspell that comes from a prayer written by St. Richard of Chichester (1197-1253) expressing his obedience to God.

Day by Day [1]

Thanks be to Thee, my Lord Jesus Christ,
for all the benefits which Thou hast given me,
for all the pains and insults Thou hast borne for me.
O most merciful Redeemer, Friend, and Brother.
May I know Thee more clearly,
love Thee more dearly,

and follow Thee more nearly,
day by day. Amen

How might a prayer like this impact your walk of obedience? Today and day by day, seek to:

- 'know him more clearly' (relationship)
- 'love him more dearly' (responsiveness)
- 'follow him more nearly' (revealing Christ)

Train Yourself

What is one of your favorite sports to watch? Who is the champion you cheer for when there's an incredible execution of a play? Consider now the daily routine and practice that went into that outcome. Even professional athletes who are 'naturals' put hours and hours into practice, taking their skills to the next level. Think of the victorious champion we could be, as a disciple of Christ, as we do our part and God does his.

How do Jesus' word in Matthew 16:24-25 come alive for you? "Whoever wants to be my disciple must deny themselves and take up their cross and follow me. For whoever wants to save their life will lose it, but whoever loses their life for me will find it."

Dietrich Bonhoeffer says, "The first Christ-suffering which every man must experience is the call to abandon the attachments of this world." [2] In Matthew 4:20, 10-11 months after his baptism, Jesus called disciples to follow, and their response was "At once they left their nets and followed him." If Jesus is saying to you, 'follow me,' what do you need to leave behind?

> *Relevant Discipleship is about becoming like Jesus, not just learning about Jesus.*
> *@nelsonroth*

Being More Like Christ

Let's get practical around the outcomes of practicing the 7 Disciplines. Here are possible results for each discipline. The five outcomes listed under each of the 7 Disciplines are actual experiences shared by those who are on a lifelong journey on the Relevant Discipleship Pathway™. What do you see active in your life right now?

Worship – experiencing God when gathered with other believers and through the week as a lifestyle.

> "praising God" Acts 2:47
> Ephesus, "forsaken their first love" Revelation 2:4

- Worship is my response, both personally and corporately, to God for who he is.
- I understand the importance of gathering regularly for worship and teaching.
- I understand I exist for God's purposes and glory.
- How I live my life daily shows I love God with all my heart.

- God has first place and is in the center of my life.

Prayer – communicating with God alone and with others.

> "They devoted themselves - to the breaking of bread and to prayer" Acts 2:42
> Smyrna, "don't be afraid - the devil will put some of you in prison to test you - be faithful" Revelation 2:10

- I understand and practice different forms of prayer – adoration, confession, thanksgiving.
- I turn to God in spontaneous prayer throughout the day.
- I regularly join in with others for prayer.
- Since prayer is communication, I take time to be silent and listen to what God has to say.
- I practice the habit of intercessory prayer, praying for others.

Word – developing a deeper relationship with God and having a passion for knowing him more.

> "They devoted themselves to the apostles' teaching" Acts 2:42
> Pergamos, "compromised their faith and needed to repent" Revelation 2:16

- I believe the Bible is the Word of God and is the authority in my life.

- I consistently pursue the habit of reading the Bible to help me become more like Jesus.
- When life changes or issues arise, I make decisions based on biblical principles.
- I actively memorize and dedicate time to reflective meditation on God's Word.
- My Bible reading and study has deepened my faith in God.

Ministry – discovering spiritual gifts and serving like Christ.

> "to give to anyone who had need" Acts 2:45
> Thyatira, "loved the world and only concerned about self" Revelation 2:20

- I know my spiritual gifts and use those gifts in ministry for the benefit of others.
- I enjoy meeting the needs of others without expecting anything in return.
- In serving, I strive to love as Jesus loved and serve as Jesus served.
- I look for new ways to serve and be missional in my community.
- I know and align with the mission and vision of the ministry I affiliate with.

Discipleship – growing godly in character with a foundation of personal values and purpose.

> "They devoted themselves" Acts 2:42

Sardis, "fallen asleep and just going through the motions" Revelation 3:2

- I understand the cost of being a disciple of Christ and am willing to die to self.
- I am a committed follower of Christ, practicing the disciplines to make room for God.
- Because it matters more "who I am," than "what I do," I am passionate about Christlikeness.
- I am able to share a clear testimony of my conversion and how I came to Christ.
- Since I've been discipled, I will engage in making disciples and the discipleship process.

Community – loving one another and sharing life.

"They devoted themselves - to fellowship" Acts 2:42
Philadelphia, "had an open door" Revelation 3:8 (philea = brotherly love)

- I am deepening my understanding of genuine relationships by fellowshipping with others.
- I live out the relational instructions of the "one anothers" in the Bible.
- When there is interpersonal conflict, I deal with it in a biblical manner.
- I regularly gather in a small group for the purpose of growing spiritually and serving.
- I meet regularly with someone for accountability and ongoing discipleship.

Evangelism – cultivating intentional friendships with not-yet believers.

> "enjoying the favor of all the people. And the Lord added to their number daily those who were being saved" Acts 2:47
> Laodecia, "lukewarm - self-sufficient and inward focused" Revelation 3:16

- I understand and am obedient to the Great Commission of going and making disciples.
- I develop friendships with not-yet believers for the purpose of being salt and light.
- I understand the Gospel, who Jesus Christ is and what he has done for sinful humankind.
- I desire and work at having an impact and positive influence in my community.
- I am eager when given an opportunity to share my conversion story.

Pause and Ponder

What discipline do you see active in your life right now?
Which outcomes challenge you to a deeper commitment level?
What transformational outcome would you add to the lists above?

Now that we've seen many transformational outcomes of discipleship, how does the following Dallas

Willard quote reinforce the importance of training and transformation for you?

We aren't born again to stay the way we are. But how many times have we looked around us in dismay at the lack of spiritual maturity in fellow believers? It is evident in the rising rate of divorces among Christian couples. We find it in the high percentages of Christians, even pastors, who regularly view pornography. And we face it each time a well-known leader in the Christian community is found in sexual sin or handling finances dishonestly. Perhaps you have struggled with your own character issues for years, even decades, to little avail. [3]

The question to ask around the 7 Disciplines is not, "Can I check it off for today?" Rather, did my activity bring me closer to God?
@nelsonroth

The final stage of the four cyclical stages of the Nehemiah Response Coaching Model™; which we use on the Relevant Discipleship Pathway™, is transformation. See a graphic of the model in the Appendix on page 177. A coaching approach to discipleship and using the stages of this model as a guide for your spiritual conversations will always emphasize transformation.

Here's what Dr. Jamie D. Aten, from the Department of Psychology at Wheaton College, had to say about the Nehemiah Response Coaching Model™ and how it relates to transformation.

> Nelson's model is a "how-to" biblical transition process. The model, integrated with social and behavioral sciences, fits well with the Transtheoretical Model which proposes how we change. What I like about the Nehemiah Response Coaching Model is that it goes beyond behavior change to transformation. [4]

Sanctification

The theological word for transformation is sanctification. Don't let a five-syllable word intimidate you. It'll be essential to understand at least its primary meaning. Let me unpack it for you.

Sanctification is the reorientation of our desires as a believer. As we choose to follow Christ, our part is obedience. Romans 6:17-18, "...you have come to obey from your heart...You have been set free from sin and have become slaves to righteousness." God's part, represents all he's done for us by 'giving his one and only son.' Galatians 2:21, "I do not set aside the grace of God, for if righteousness could be gained through the law, Christ died for nothing!"

God's Part

God's grace takes the initiative first to pursue a relationship with us. God then responds in grace to those who turn to him in repentance with forgiveness and restoration. Then sanctifying grace moves us on toward perfection.

By God's grace, salvation is in three parts - past, present, and future. We are saved from the penalty, power, and presence of sin. Here are three theological words to become familiar with: justification, sanctification, and glorification. Let's take a more in-depth look at each of these words.

Justification is being made right with God based on Christ's righteousness. Justification takes care of the past, and we are saved from the penalty of sin. It makes it 'just-as-if' we have never sinned (Romans 3:23-24).

Sanctification is the same word in the Bible as holiness. It means separation of yourself unto God. First, for the believer, there is a once-for-all positional separation unto Christ at our salvation. Secondly, there is a practical, progressive separation or holiness in a believer's life while waiting for the return of Christ. Sanctification here is about our present situation as a follower of Christ, and we gain victory over the power of sin (2 Corinthians 5:21; 1 Thessalonians 5:23).

Glorification will be experienced in heaven when Christians who are now burdened with the possibility of still sinning become holy immortals. Glorification will be experienced in the future, and we will be delivered or saved from the very presence of sin (Romans 5:2).

I heard it like this once...as followers, we practice our position. Sanctification is the positional work of God where the believer is righteous in Christ; and, the ongoing work of God to progressively conform a believer to Christ. As believers, we are each responsible for this ongoing sanctification. Sanctification is practicing or living out, our position.

So, in this matter of living a holy life and sanctification, there are two kinds of righteousness... positional and practical. As we strive to be more like Christ in this present life, let me explain the difference.

> **Positional**, imputed righteousness where God views us as righteous because of Christ, and we are forgiven..."God made him who had no sin to be sin for us, so that in him we might become the righteousness of God." (2 Corinthians 5:21)

> **Practical righteousness**, holy living and putting off sin..."Whoever wants to be my disciple must deny themselves and take up their cross daily and follow me." (Luke 9:23)

In his book, *The Pursuit of Holiness*, chapter ten titled, "The Place of Personal Discipline," Jerry Bridges wrote..."Discipline toward holiness begins then with the Scriptures...The Holy Spirit has already done a good part of His work by providing us with the Scriptures to discipline us. And as we learn them, He will faithfully bring them to our minds as we need them to face temptations. As we seek to apply His Word to daily situations, He will work in us to strengthen us." [5]

"Do not conform to the pattern of this world, but be transformed by the renewing of your mind. Then you will be able to test and approve what God's will is—his good, pleasing and perfect will" (Romans 12:2).

Ephesians 4:11-13, "So Christ himself gave the apostles, the prophets, the evangelists, the pastors and teachers, to equip his people for works of service, so that the body of Christ may be built up until we all reach unity in the faith and in the knowledge of the Son of God and become mature, attaining to the whole measure of the fullness of Christ."

Pause and Ponder

How could revitalization and transformation come about in our churches?
What is your individual part?
What impact would a transformational, multiplying discipleship process integrated into the life of your church have?

Transformation begins and continues with the partnership of the Holy Spirit. As a believer, he lives in you and is the provider of the power source needed. Let's get ready for the next chapter about the Holy Spirit by reading Paul's prayer for the Ephesian church:

For this reason, ever since I heard about your faith in the Lord Jesus and your love for all God's people, I have not stopped giving thanks for you, remembering you in my prayers. I keep asking that the God of our Lord Jesus Christ, the glorious Father, **may give you the Spirit of wisdom and revelation, so that you may know him better.** I pray that the eyes of your heart may be enlightened in order that you may **know the hope to which he has called you, the riches of his glorious inheritance in his holy people, and his incomparably great power for us who believe.** That **power is the same as the mighty strength he exerted when he raised Christ from the dead** and seated him at his right hand in the heavenly realms, far above all rule and authority, power and dominion, and every name that is invoked, not only in the present age but also in the one to come. And God placed all things under his feet **and appointed him to be head over everything for the church, which is his**

body, the fullness of him who fills everything in every way. (Ephesians 1:15-23, emphasis added)

"That power is the same as the mighty strength he exerted when he raised Christ from the dead..." What transformational outcomes are you noticing God is bringing about in your life?

what leaders are saying...

I found the Relevant Discipleship Pathway so powerful and life giving. The discipleship resources are interesting and thought provoking. The 7 Disciplines offered me a chance to explore more fully my own discipleship path. The individual discipleship coaching was such a gift and Pam's warm approach and attentive listening gave me such freedom to be truthful in so many ways.

—Rev. Kim Alexander
Horison Methodist Church
Johannesburg, South Africa

Over the six months, I worked with Pam on the Relevant Discipleship Pathway, it caused me to realize for the last two years, I have been living Romans 12:2. Although I have probably read that scripture many times before, this time it was like an "ah ha moment!" I finally came to the realization that God was transforming me by the 'Renewing of My Mind.' I get it! And the transformation came through the Relevant Discipleship Pathway and experiencing Discipleship Coaching, I can look at each discipline and realize that even though I was doing many of these disciplines already, I have a much greater awareness and appreciation. Working with Pam has made me much more intentional and focused on what God is calling me to do. I have grown in my prayer life, am now meditating every morning, learning scripture, reading God's word, devoted to service in my church, and committed to bringing others to Christ.

—Julie Gallagher-Gough, ACC
Keller, TX

The Relevant Discipleship Pathway is transformational. The well thought out process is a wonderful journey that begins with identifying the core aspects of discipleship and ends with an overall plan to create a discipleship culture within one's own ministry context. If you have a desire to make, equip, and multiply Christian disciples then the Relevant

Discipleship Pathway is for you. I wish I would have discovered Relevant Discipleship years ago. The discipleship coaching training and one-to-one sessions were transformational. The concise discipleship pathway, relevant resources and Nehemiah Response Coaching Model have focused my personal growth as a disciple and provided the tools necessary to foster a culture of discipleship within my ministry.

— Dr. Abe Smith, Minister
First United Methodist Church
Allen, TX

The Relevant Discipleship Pathway is a descriptive way of understanding how each person is invited to move from viewing faith to abiding in God's presence. And yet, that's not the final chapter. The pathway leads us into the presence of God, transforms and sends us forth to minister to others. For those of us who are United Methodist, it gives us the tools to intentionally fulfill our stated mission: "Make disciples for Jesus Christ for the transformation of the world.

— Rena Yocom
Missiologist, Theological educator, and
Retired clergy in UMC
Edgerton, KS

7 the Holy Spirit

Resurrection day was an important marker on the discipleship pathway for Jesus' followers. As I'm writing, I just reread John chapter twenty, and I'm stirred in my spirit with the account of the events of the day.

I want to share what happened, when Jesus gathered with his disciples, on the Sunday night of resurrection day. Understanding what happened that night will make all the difference in your journey on the discipleship pathway. Before you read on with what I have written, I'd like to suggest putting this book down and opening your Bible to John twenty and reading the chapter first. As you do...the part I want to focus on from John's account of the resurrection of Christ is when Jesus appeared to his disciples for the first time in the Upper Room. It's in verses nineteen to twenty-two.

> *Relevant Discipleship is a judgement-free safe place where two people get real with each other and the Holy Spirit works.* @nelsonroth

Receive the Holy Spirit

"On the evening of the first day of the week, when the disciples were together, with the doors locked for fear of the Jewish leaders, ...Jesus came and stood among them and said, 'Peace be with you!' After he said this, he showed them his hands and side. The disciples were overjoyed when they saw the Lord. Again Jesus said, 'Peace be with you! As the Father has sent me, I am sending you.' And with that he breathed on them and said, 'Receive the Holy Spirit'" (John 20:19-22).

The statement, "I am sending you," in the book of John is the same Great Commission that we are more familiar with in Matthew 28:19, "Therefore go and make disciples…" After Jesus said, "I am sending you." He "breathed on them and said, 'Receive the Holy Spirit.'" As we are "sent" and as we "go and make disciples" what's your source of power for discipleship and disciple-making?

Having the necessary power in our Christian life is essential. Who can drive a car without an engine? Without an electrical outlet, how can a lamp provide us with light? How can this computer I'm using operate without keeping the battery charged?

Promise of the Spirit

In John 14, just a few days before the night of the resurrection, the disciples were given an extraordinary promise. In John 14:16-17, Jesus said, "...I will ask the Father, and he will give you another advocate to help you and be with you forever—the Spirit of truth." Then, he continues in verse seventeen, saying, "...for he lives with you and will be in you." Both statements speak of a future happening. And it happened on resurrection night, when Christ "breathed on them and said, 'Receive the Holy Spirit.'"

This day also marked the beginning of the New Covenant. Though Jesus' ministry and training of the disciples take place in the New Testament, Jesus and his disciples were still under the Old Covenant of the Old Testament. The New Covenant of salvation through the sacrifice of Christ on the cross began with the resurrection at the end of the Gospels and the beginning of Acts.

As we consider our source of power for discipleship and disciple-making, what does the 'breathing and receiving the Holy Spirit' mean for us today as disciples? Let's take a moment to focus in on what happened in John 20:22.

Jesus "breathed on them." In the original language 'breathed' is the same Greek word used in Genesis 2:7 in the Septuagint, the Koine Greek translation of a Hebraic text of the Old Testament. This verse tells us, "...God formed a man from the dust of the ground and breathed into his nostrils the breath of life, and the man became a living being." So, just as the original creation happened by an act of God, the new creation and indwelling of the Holy Spirit are initiated by an act of Jesus Christ. The disciples were at that moment indwelt with the Holy Spirit. Christ "breathed on them and said, 'Receive the Holy Spirit.'"

The Holy Spirit was the source of power for the original disciples of Christ. As Christ's disciples today, our source of power is the same. Being and making disciples requires the Spirit's power. We can't force or manufacture discipleship in our own strength. With this in mind, how do the following two shifts for discipleship on the pathway challenge you?

- Shifting from being transactional to being transformational because we are a new creation in Christ, and operating in the Spirit's power.
- Shifting from doing to being, so that we are a light revealing Christ that others notice. "Always be prepared to give an answer to everyone who asks you to give the reason for the hope that you have" as the Spirit gives opportunity. (1 Peter 3:15)

Two Extremes

These two shifts give us as disciples and disciple makers insight regarding our methods and the source of our power. What's your experience around the subject of the Holy Spirit? Often it seems it's all or not at all when it comes to a relationship with the Holy Spirit. If we have any hesitations about a relationship with the Holy Spirit, Martyn Lloyd-Jones can help us think this through and overcome our concerns.

In his book, *Joy Unspeakable*, Martyn Lloyd-Jones says, "There are two main ways in which, it seems to me, we can go wrong in this question of the relationship of our experiences to the teaching of the Scripture (about the Spirit)." [1] Martyn Lloyd-Jones is talking about two extremes possible in our relationship with the Holy Spirit...let me call it, overuse and underuse of the Holy Spirit.

If we need the Spirit's power, wouldn't it be essential to get this right? What's the healthy balance about the truth of the Spirit's work in our lives? Wouldn't it be just like the evil one to confuse us in this matter if it is that the Spirit's power working in and through us is imperative? Martyn Lloyd-Jones explains further by writing about these two extremes he calls dangers:

> The first danger is that of claiming things which either go beyond Scripture or which, indeed, may even be contrary to it...I remember once hearing a man saying he did not care what the apostle Paul or anybody else said, he knew! He had had an experience. Now the moment a man says that, he is putting his own experience above Scriptures. That opens the door to fanaticism, not enthusiasm but fanaticism and other possible dangers.

> So there is one danger...when we put what we experience subjectively over the Scripture. Another way in which this is

done is to put tradition or the teaching of the church above Scripture.

The second (danger) is the exact opposite of the first, as these things generally go from one violent extreme to the other. How difficult it always is to maintain a balance! The second danger, then, is that of being satisfied with something very much less than what is offered in the Scripture, and the danger of interpreting Scripture by our experiences and reducing its teaching to the level of what we know and experience; and I would say that this second is the greater danger of the two at the present time.

In other words, certain people by nature are afraid of the supernatural, of the unusual, of disorder. You can be so afraid of disorder...that you become guilty of what the Scripture calls 'quenching the Spirit;' and there is no question in my mind that there has been a great deal of this.

People come to the New Testament and, instead of taking its teaching as it is, they interpret it in the light of their experience, and so they reduce it. Everything is explained regarding what they have and what they experience. And I believe that this is very largely responsible for the condition of the Christian church at this present time. [2]

On resurrection day, Jesus "breathed on them, and said, 'Receive the Holy Spirit.'" He said, take or receive the Holy Spirit. In the language in the New Testament, the verb, receive, is in the aorist tense, and it's imperative. Aorist, meaning 'right now,' take the Holy Spirit I'm breathing into you. The night of the resurrection, the disciples were indwelt with the Holy Spirit! Jesus gives them the Holy Spirit to empower them to do what he was commissioning them to do.

> *Being a disciple takes us beyond our level of comfort where the only thing we can do is depend on God. @nelsonroth*

From resurrection night forward, at conversion, those who believe in Christ are indwelt with the Spirit. Here's what the Apostle Paul had to say to believers who were still struggling with fleshly habits and temptations, "Do you not know that your bodies are temples of the Holy Spirit, who is in you, whom you have received from God?" (1 Corinthians 6:19).

Indwelt, Baptized or Filled, Walk or Live

Let's pause, take a deep breath, and to help bring clarity, consider the different designations of the working of the Holy Spirit in the lives of a believer.

There are three different designations in the New Testament that describe the believer's relationship with the Holy Spirit and each one has a different meaning which is vital to understand. The three designations are indwelt with the Spirit, baptized or filled with the Spirit, and walk or live in the Spirit.

Just before his death and resurrection, Jesus taught his disciples about the promise of the Holy Spirit. John 14:15-17, "If you love me, keep my commands. And I will ask the Father, and he will give you another advocate to help you and be with you forever—the Spirit of truth. The world cannot accept him, because it neither sees him nor knows him. But you know him, for he lives with you and will be in you."

Today as disciples and followers of Christ, knowing we are indwelt with the Holy Spirit is essential. On the day of our salvation, when we receive Christ as our Savior, the Holy Spirit indwells us.

The Trinity

Let's add some background to the work of the Holy Spirit by considering who he is. The Spirit is the third person of the Trinity. 2 Corinthians 13:14 says, "May the grace of the Lord Jesus Christ, and the love of God, and the fellowship of the Holy Spirit be with you all." The Holy Spirit is not a shadow or an impersonal force. He is a person, equal in every way with the Father and the Son, Jesus Christ. All of the divine attributes ascribed to the Father and Son are also ascribed to the

Holy Spirit. The Father, Son, and Spirit are one; and yet, they each have distinct roles.

Holy Spirit and Old Covenant

Next, we learn the Holy Spirit, like God, has existed since the beginning. In Genesis 1:1 we read, "In the beginning God created the heavens and the earth...and the Spirit of God was hovering over the waters." In the Old Testament, the Holy Spirit was active as he came upon certain people at different times for specific purposes to serve God. The significant difference between the Old and the New Covenant is in the Old Covenant, the Spirit came upon certain people at different times, and in the New Covenant, the Spirit indwells every believer.

Here are several examples of the Spirit during Old Covenant times coming upon certain people. Pharaoh, said this about Joseph, "Can we find anyone like this man, one in whom is the Spirit of God?" (Genesis 41:38). And, David said in 2 Samuel 23:2, "The Spirit of the Lord spoke through me; his word was on my tongue." When Jesus began his ministry in John 1:32-33, John the Baptist said, "I saw the Spirit descend from heaven as a dove and remain on him...the one who sent me to baptize with water said to me, 'The man on whom you see the Spirit come down and remain is the one who will baptize with the Holy Spirit.'"

Holy Spirit and New Covenant

Moving forward to the New Testament, or specifically, the New Covenant, the Spirit's first work in the lives of all people is conviction and drawing not-yet believers to Christ. Since the resurrection of Jesus, the Holy Spirit's initial role in the lives of people is to cause them to be aware of their need for salvation. "When he comes, he will prove the world to be in the wrong about sin and righteousness and judgment" (John 16:8).

Then, when a person accepts Jesus Christ as Lord and Savior, he or she is indwelt with the Holy Spirit. Right then, right there in a nanosecond. The person opens his or her heart to Christ, Jesus breaths, and the Holy Spirit indwells him or her.

Here are some verses that give certainty for this reality of the indwelling of the Holy Spirit.

> Romans 8:9, "…if anyone does not have the Spirit of Christ, they do not belong to Christ."

> Galatians 4:6, "Because you are sons, God sent the Spirit of his Son into our hearts…"

> 1 Corinthians 6:19, "Do you not know that your bodies are temples of the Holy Spirit, who is in you, whom you have received from God?"

Since the resurrection of Christ, when a person receives Christ, the Holy Spirit immediately indwells the believer. Consider the following three verses that come before and after the resurrection. The first two are pre-resurrection and the third is post-resurrection.

> John 7:37-39, "...Up to that time the Spirit had not been given, since Jesus had not yet been glorified." [pre-resurrection]

> John 14:17, "...for he lives with you, and will be in you." [pre-resurrection]

> John 20:22, Christ "breathed on them and said, 'Receive the Holy Spirit.'" [post-resurrection]

I hope this is helpful to you in understanding the work of the Holy Spirit following conviction. He indwells those who receive Christ as Savior. Next, let's look into the baptism or the filling of the Spirit.

Bring Baptized or Filled With the Spirit

Is it possible for a believer to be indwelt but not baptized or filled with the Spirit? Let's read Acts 1:5. Jesus said, "For John baptized with water, but in a few days you will be baptized with the Holy Spirit." Remember believers were indwelt with the Spirit on resurrection day. Acts 1:8 reads, "But you will receive power when the Holy Spirit comes on you." These verses refer to what happened in Acts 2:4, "All of them were all filled with the Holy Spirit..." So, there is an initial Spirit baptism or filling. It is a separate event and may or may not happen simultaneously with salvation and the Spirit's indwelling. As a fully devoted follower of Christ, when we're yielded or fully surrendered to the Holy Spirit, he is not only in us; but also on us for works of service.

With Spirit baptism or filling, there is an initial event when Jesus becomes the Lord of our life and this is to be followed by an ongoing experience. Ephesians 5:18, "...be filled with the Spirit." The reference to filling here is in the present tense and it's to be continuous. Literally, 'keep on, continually being filled or under the control of the Holy Spirit.'

> Discipleship is about becoming like Christ. We do that by the indwelling Spirit, not by our doing. Relevant Discipleship is about abiding.
> @nelsonroth

Believers are indwelt when they receive Christ. The Spirit comes upon believers for power and service when they've experienced baptism and they continue to be filled with the Spirit. Then, the third designation is walk in or live in the Spirit. This is the life lived by a spirit-filled believer spoken of in Galatians 5:16, "walk by (live-in) the Spirit."

Walk By or Live in the Spirit

The Holy Spirit indwells you. Power for service comes with being continually filled and living in the Spirit. You have all of the Holy Spirit if you are a believer. The pertinent question to ask now is... "Does the Holy Spirit have all of me?"

The understanding of these three different designations is essential in the believer's relationship with the Holy Spirit. Believers are:

- Indwelt immediately at their salvation
- To surrender and be filled
- To continually walk in the Spirit; living a godly life and serving effectively

Pause and Ponder

How does the understanding of these three designations help you?
How is God through the Spirit's work prompting you right now?

The power of the Spirit is God's promise and gift. He is the giver, and we are the receiver by yielding to the Holy Spirit's indwelling presence. Luke 11:13 says, "...how much more will your Father in heaven give the Holy Spirit to those who ask him!"

By My Witnesses

What is the purpose of having the power of the Spirit in and on our lives? It certainly isn't about something spectacular that we do. The purpose of the presence and power of the Spirit in the believer's life is found in Acts 1:8. "But you will receive power when the Holy Spirit comes on you; and you will be my witnesses in Jerusalem, and in all Judea and Samaria, and to the ends of the earth." The purpose of having this power is making disciples!

> A spiritual journey integrated with Relevant Discipleship helps you discover your mission in the world. @nelsonroth

In his book, *Absolute Surrender*, Andrew Murray says, "And lest anyone should have a wrong impression as to what it is to be filled with the Spirit, just let me say that it does not mean a state of high excitement or absolute perfection. No. Being filled with the Spirit is simply this - having my whole nature yielded to His power. When the whole soul yields to the Holy Spirit, God Himself will fill it." [3]

what leaders are saying...

> Relevant Discipleship was the nudge I needed to go back to seven basic themes that should be a part of every Christ follower. Spending three weeks focusing on each discipline and then talking about it with Nelson reinforced what I had learned; and, with the coaching approach I was challenged to take my next steps. It was the intentional process that made it possible to focus and pray for the Holy Spirit to open my spiritual eyes about the discipline I was working on. God would always show me a new insight and would invite me where He was already at work.

My vision for our church is to create a culture where talking about Jesus is as easy as talking about hobbies over a meal or a cup of coffee.

—Bob Depew, Pastor
Way of Life Community Church
Mobile, AL

I was immensely impressed when I learned about the Relevant Discipleship Pathway. The content includes a deep dive into the discipleship process and how to systematise the introduction of such processes into one-to-one work; as well as, assisting leaders of the church to introduce the concepts to their congregations through a coaching approach. My vision is to evolve my coaching practice to implement a coaching approach to discipleship that encourages the coachee to have living contact with the Holy Spirit and as such to receive, as a product of grace, catalytic revelation.

—Richard Thorby ACC, MBA (IMD)
Matrix Consulting UK Ltd
Executive Coach
Horsham, England, UK

8 resources to get started

You have decided to be discipled or maybe you are ready to disciple someone using a coaching approach, and to get on the discipleship pathway. So, what's the next step? While you're experiencing discipleship, you have the Relevant Discipleship Pathway™ and the Nehemiah Response Coaching Model™ as tools to help with knowing 'what to do' and 'what to say.' But, what resources would you use within this pathway of the 7 Disciplines we're learning to practice? Here's where we must be careful not to slip back into our ministry program tendencies. In this chapter we want to distinguish between:

- Program vs Process
- Curriculum vs Content
- Classes to complete vs a Lifelong journey

As you may have guessed, the Relevant Discipleship Pathway™ embraces the last word in each of the three sets of words above. It's a **process**, allowing for the Spirit to put his finger on the right **content** to practice the disciplines as we as disciples walk the **lifelong journey** of following and becoming more like Christ.

Here's a powerful statement about practicing the behavior of effective disciple-making from Greg Ogden.

> Programs promote a classroom setting with many people involved, and the focus is on gaining knowledge which sometimes never gets used in life. In a program, accountability is low, and the commitment to finishing the course is greater than the commitment to actually practice the behaviors of effective disciple-making. [1]

Process

With the Relevant Discipleship Pathway™, we have developed content for a six-month journey. The materials compiled in the *Relevant Discipleship™ Resource Manual* compliment the pathway. We will share more in this chapter about the content for you as you are experiencing the pathway and coaching approach to this lifelong discipleship journey.

The primary objective of the pathway is experiencing God, so think of the resources in the *Relevant Discipleship™ Resource Manual* as the instrument that encourages and fosters this activity. The resources in the manual are not to be the end all be all. And, once the framework of the pathway becomes a familiar part of your life's journey, it will apply to what other materials and Christian books have to offer. The framework will be the system or skeletal structure that supports your ongoing, growing spiritual life.

> The 7 Disciplines of Relevant Discipleship are interrelated, development in one discipline has positive impact on the others. @nelsonroth

You can most certainly come back to the *Relevant Discipleship™ Resource Manual* repeatedly. Pick it up and use it as the Holy Spirit leads you on your journey. In addition to the *Relevant Discipleship™ Resource Manual*, consider all of the books you have on your shelves as another way you might practice any of the 7 Disciplines of a disciple at various times on your lifelong journey. By continually applying new material to the pathway, the process is ongoing and becomes a way of life for the rest of your life. Remember, the *Relevant Discipleship™ Resource Manual* is an essential tool for your first time through. It will also help those you disciple have a foundational start on their journey.

Content: Articles, Coaching Tools, and Lessons

There are three categories in the manual. For each of the 7 Disciplines, there are four short articles and a coaching tool. There is also a lesson that's either part of the one-to-one discipleship sessions or the lessons can be used by the leader of a small group that's embracing the Relevant Discipleship Pathway™. We refer to these small group leaders as Culture Changers. Culture

Changers in regards to developing a discipleship culture within their small group or on a larger scale, their church.

When a disciplee chooses the discipline to focus on for the next three weeks between his or her one-to-one sessions, he or she reads and applies the particular articles and coaching tool for that discipline. The articles are written with specific themes around the 3Rs. The first of each of the four articles is about the discipline, in particular. Then, the next three articles are purposefully designed around the discipline and the themes of relationship, being responsive and revealing Christ. The coaching tool is full of powerful questions and can be incorporated in a person's time with God by using a self-coaching technique of asking questions with anticipation of how God might show up.

The only variable in the nonlinear approach to the *Relevant Disciple™ Resource Manual* is the lessons. They are in sequential order and are to be used for each one-to-one discipleship session or small group gathering. The 7 Disciplines are nonlinear on purpose. The discipline is chosen by the disciplee related to what might be most helpful for them to focus on next, so with that being said, the 7 Disciplines can be practiced in any order.

Remember in chapter five when we referred to the way Jesus taught his disciples? When they asked 'how to pray' he did not say, "Hey guys, that's in chapter eight and we'll get to that in three weeks." No, he responded right there and then to their question. During the three weeks of focus, remember, it's not about mastering the discipline; instead, it's about seeing what God is showing you and discovering what your next steps on the pathway might be. During a particular focus, the other disciplines are not disregarded; rather, that particular focus is essential for those specific three weeks. Then at the end of the first six months, a healthy balance of all of the disciplines is in place as we continue the lifelong journey in various ways; allowing God's leading in the practice of the 7 Disciplines.

> *One-to-one discipleship works. God created us for mutual interdependence. "Iron sharpens iron." (Proverbs 27:17) @nelsonroth*

Lifelong Journey: Experiencing the Pathway

This first six-month period on the Relevant Discipleship Pathway™ is sort of like a 'boot camp' for being a disciple. It is a great start for believers to begin an intentional and transformational walk with Jesus. As this walk of being a disciple continues, making disciples becomes the organic outcome. Interestingly, this first six-month period has been a blessing not only for laity; but, also for leaders of churches. It's an opportunity for what some leaders have said, "To be able to practice what they preach." If discipleship is to be a movement, what better place to begin than with the leaders.

Here's what some leaders have had to say about their personal experience:

Spending time focusing on the 7 Disciplines with my Relevant Discipleship Coach has energized and deepened my own relationship with God. (church leader from Texas)

I have experienced a wonderful new opportunity to learn and grow in my own walk with Christ as well as to share His love through Discipleship Coaching. (church leader from Missouri)

I felt God moving me to bring discipleship into my church; yet, realizing that I had never REALLY been discipled myself. My regular coaching conversations led to some amazing shifts in my heart and a deeper connection to the Almighty God. (church leader from New Jersey)

Discipleship Coaching and engaging in the Relevant Discipleship Pathway has brought me back to the basics. (church leader from Arkansas)

Relevant Discipleship has been a breath of fresh air for me. For so long, I've been giving out. Through the one-to-one discipleship relationship and my time with the Lord; prayer, time of devotion and study is more meaningful and exciting. (church leader from Mississippi)

The Relevant Discipleship Pathway was the nudge I needed to go back to basic themes that should be a part of every Christ follower.

Spending three weeks focusing on each discipline and then talking about it reinforced what I had learned; and, with the coaching approach, I was challenged to take my next steps. (church leader from Alabama)

The Relevant Discipleship process has been a tremendous catalyst for my spiritual growth. It was a challenging, enjoyable journey that continues to this day. (church leader from Mississippi)

As I have worked through the seven disciplines, I have never failed to experience both insight and steps of positive growth. This was particularly true in the disciplines of prayer and ministry. Both of these areas of my spiritual life have been strengthened. (church leader from Illinois)

The Relevant Discipleship process has personally helped me gain some direction and understanding about what discipleship may look like for me, my church, and my community. (church leader from Illinois)

The Relevant Discipleship one-to-one sessions helped me to have an accountable person. To know there is someone, I'm in relationship with, provides the encouragement I need. I'm excited about what is happening in my life and my church around discipleship. (church leader from Louisiana)

The Relevant Discipleship process impacted me personally by having someone there who cared enough about my spiritual growth to connect with me one-to-one, providing accountability in an environment where I could be real about my walk with Christ. (church leader from Mississippi)

> *When Christian leadership and ministry responsibility precedes discipleship, burn-out or bail-out down the road is more likely to occur. @nelsonroth*

Relevant Discipleship™ is a relational process where two people commit to meet; welcoming the Holy Spirit to guide in each meeting. There is a suggested six-month period, meeting every three weeks intentionally around the 7 Disciplines of a disciple.

Pause and Ponder

How does experiencing the Relevant Discipleship Pathway™ sound to you?
If you're on the journey, how is it going?
If you're hearing all of this for the first time, when would you like to get started?

One-to-One

Here's a helpful overview of the pathway process, using the *Relevant Discipleship™ Resource Manual*:

- A one-to-one relationship is formed for a period of six months to practice the 7 Disciplines. (This is highly effective within a small group or class setting.)
- As the disciplee, you choose one of the 7 Disciplines to focus on for three weeks.
- You may pick a discipline in any order.
- Set a time and place to meet for the next session.
- During your personal time of reflection, focus on your chosen discipline:

  ...use the four articles and coaching tool for the particular discipline in your *Relevant Discipleship™ Resource Manual.*

  ...rather than mastering a particular discipline during the three weeks, remember the purpose is discovering "what God wants to teach you and what your next step is around that discipline as a Christ follower."
- At the end of each discipleship session, choose another discipline to focus on for the next three weeks until you have practiced all 7 Disciplines.
- At the end of your six-month journey together, multiply by discipling someone else with the same process you have experienced.

The *Relevant Discipleship™ Resource Manual* and *Nehemiah Response: a coaching model* are available at Amazon.com. For information about quantity discounts, contact us at Relevant Ministry (contact@relevantministry.org).

9 making room to experience God

How might the child's game of 'hot and cold' get us thinking about experiencing God and making room to do so? Do you remember how to play the game? You hide something and give the person you're playing the game with signals by saying 'hot or cold' to direct the person to the object. As they get closer and closer, you call out, "you're getting hotter and hotter," until they find it.

Brother Lawrence is someone we all can learn from in this matter of experiencing God. Three hundred years ago, he was a kitchen worker in a monastery in Paris. He didn't have the theological training like the monks he cooked for; however, the monks looked to him because of his spirituality. When he wasn't working, Brother Lawrence would write letters to those who would ask him questions about his close relationship with God. Those letters were compiled, after his death, into a little book titled, *The Practice of the Presence of*

God; and, it is a classic today. The following paragraph is a short section out of the book.

> To be with Him, we must cultivate the holy habit of thinking of Him often. You will tell me that I always say the same thing. What can I say? It is true. I don't know an easier method, nor do I practice any other, so I advise this one to everybody. We have to know someone before we can truly love them. In order to know God, we must think about Him often. And once we get to know Him, we will think about Him even more often, because where our treasure is, there also is our heart! [1]

Practice of the Presence

"The holy habit of thinking of Him often." For Brother Lawrence, practicing being in the presence of God was a twenty-four seven habit. Even during his kitchen work, he wrote about how he did not let the noise from the clanging of the pots and pans or anything else be a distraction from focusing on the presence of God in his life. So, let's go back to the child's game of 'hot or cold.' It's apparent Brother Lawrence was 'hot' in his pursuit of God.

As a disciplee on the Relevant Discipleship Pathway™, you will have the opportunity to work through a lesson with your discipler called, "Practicing the presence" in the *Relevant Discipleship™ Resource*

Manual. Or if you are in a small group while you're practicing the 7 Disciplines, this lesson will be one of twelve lessons you will study.

The Holy Habit of Thinking of Him Often

Let's pause and think about Brother Lawrence's use of the word habit. Remember the 'flatware story' in chapter five? We acknowledged that as humans, we're creatures of habit. Those habits can be good or bad. Also, new habits take time and a conscious effort to develop. As we consider our part in experiencing God; being 'hot' in our pursuit of God, there are two important words...'practice' and 'discipline.' The significant outcome is when we practice a discipline, we form new and better habits as a follower of Christ.

Putting Off Putting On

In the Bible, Paul refers to practicing the discipline of becoming more like Christ using the picture of 'putting off, renewing your mind, and putting on.' In Ephesians 4:22-24 we read, "You were taught, with regard to your former way of life, to put off your old self, which is being corrupted by its deceitful desires; to be made new in the attitude of your minds; and to put on the new self, created to be like God in true righteousness and holiness." Then in Colossians 3:9-10 Paul says, "...since you have taken off your old self with its practices and have put on the new self, which is being renewed in knowledge in the image of its Creator."

How is Paul helping you to have a better understanding of the importance of a conscious decision to practice right actions? So as a disciple walking the discipleship pathway, you can make conscious choices to intentionally practice a discipline in a particular way to form new habits.

Coaching and Contextualization

When it comes to forming new habits, it is essential for a person to discover their best approach. By taking a coaching approach to discipleship, we can listen deeply, then ask powerful questions. Remember, the disciplee is on a journey, and our role as a discipler is to provide the space they need to make the discovery. When we get out of the way, by not telling the person how you would do it or how they ought to practice the discipline, we are allowing the Holy Spirit to direct them. Telling, rather than the coaching approach may be one of the biggest hindrances in our discipleship efforts. Coaching is going to bring to light for the disciplee and you the disciple maker 'where the person is' in their relationship with God...that's contextualization and allowing new habits that are relevant to be formed by the disciplee.

> *Coaching helps contextualize where the person you're discipling is around the practice of the spiritual disciplines. @nelsonroth*

Here's a true story around contextualization and using the coaching approach for relevant new habits to be formed. I was discipling someone who chose Prayer as his next discipline of focus. So, I asked, "What would you like for prayer to look like over the next three weeks?" Do you know what he said? "I want to be an example to my family and begin to pray again before meals." Wow! That was not at all what I was expecting him to say. If it were up to me to prescribe for him a way to practice prayer for the next three weeks, I would have never suggested that. I might have recommended setting the alarm a half hour earlier to spend that half hour with God to start his day. Now, my friend may do something like that in the future; but at that particular time in his life, praying before meals with his family was the right practice of the discipline of Prayer. And, by practicing prayer before meals with his family, new habits were formed and he experienced God!

Looking back over the years, I wonder how many times while I was disciplining someone I blew them out of the water because I suggested that they should fast, or pray certain times for specific lengths of time, etc. Consider the two different scenarios of the disciplee in the previous story. What do you think would have happened if I had given him instructions to set his alarm for an earlier wake-up time? More than likely, he would have felt like a solution had been imposed on him; and would have become discouraged by the fourth or fifth day when he shut the alarm off and pulled up the covers. However, because praying before meals was what was relevant to him at the time, and it was his plan; he felt empowered as he carried through the practice of his plan successfully.

Being Disciplined

Henri Nouwen writes about experiencing God through the disciplines in an article originally published in *Leadership Journal* in 1995. The article, "From Solitude to Community to Ministry," is on the top forty list of articles published in *Leadership Journal*. Here's what Nouwen has to say about discipleship, being 'hot,' in our pursuit of experiencing God.

> The word discipleship and the word discipline is the same word, which has always fascinated me. Once you have made the choice to say, "Yes, I want to follow Jesus," the question is, "What disciplines will help me remain faithful to that choice?" If we want to be disciples of Jesus, we have to live a disciplined life.
>
> By discipline, I do not mean control. If I know the discipline of psychology or economics, I have a certain control over a

body of knowledge. If I discipline my children, I want to have a little control over them.

But in the spiritual life, the word discipline means "the effort to create some space in which God can act." Discipline means to prevent everything in your life from being filled up. [2]

How are you at practicing the holy habit of making room to experience God? Let me ask another question. It's sort of like the 'hot or cold' example I gave at the beginning of the chapter. Where is Jesus in your life? What would you hear, 'hot or cold,' from someone who knew you well?

> The spiritual discipline you're practicing at a particular time does not transform you; it makes room for a deeper relationship with God. @nelsonroth

Where is Jesus

In Luke 2:41-52, we read the story of Jesus going to the temple with his family and friends when he was twelve. This journey was an annual trip to celebrate the Feast of the Passover. The ninety miles from Nazareth, where Jesus and his family lived, to Jerusalem took around thirty hours to walk. So in the account of Jesus and his family going to Jerusalem, they spent a few days celebrating; however, something interesting happened on the way home. After a day's journey, the Scripture tells us in Luke 2:43-44, Jesus' parents discovered Jesus was missing! You might be asking, "How does that happen?" "What kind of parents were Mary and Joseph?" What do you think were some of the assumptions that everyone was making about him being left behind? Whatever the reason, it took a day to notice that Jesus was missing. Practically, we can apply this spiritually to our situations by asking:

- Where is Jesus in my life?
- What are my assumptions about Jesus?
- How long has Jesus been missing?

It is interesting to follow along with the story and to see what happens next. After the discovery of their twelve-year-old son missing, Jesus' parents began the journey back to Jerusalem. In Luke 2:46, we see it took Joseph and Mary three days to finally find Jesus. What's the spiritual implication in this account regarding your walk with Jesus? Is it possible that it is three times harder to get back in a relationship with Jesus, once we realize he's missing?

Pause and Ponder

What's your biggest challenge to stay connected with Jesus?
How does being busy or being preoccupied get in the way?
What's your self-care issue to overcome the busyness?

One of the 7 Disciplines of a disciple is Discipleship. It's about 'being a disciple.' Meaning, what really matters is 'who you are' before 'what you do.' The short definition of Discipleship on the Relevant Discipleship Pathway™ is growing godly in character with a foundation of personal values and purpose. The discipline of Discipleship is rooted in Acts 2:42, where it says the members of the early church "...devoted themselves to the apostles' teaching."

How might devotion, commitment, growing in character, and a focus on who we are instead what we are doing help us to remain in and experience God? Abiding in God is an invitation to be sanctified and live a holy life! In Ephesians 5:1-2, we are asked to "Follow God's example, therefore, as dearly loved children. And live a life of love..." In 1 Peter 1:13-16, we are commanded to be holy, "Therefore, with minds that are alert and fully sober, set your hope on the grace to be brought to you when Jesus Christ is revealed at his coming. As obedient children, do not conform to the evil desires you had when you lived in ignorance. But just as he who called you is holy, so be holy in all you do; for it is written: 'Be holy, because I am holy.'"

Pause and Ponder

Why would living a holy life be so important?
As you consider your spiritual walk right now,
are you 'hot or cold'?

Climbing the Holy Hill

Consider these things in Psalm 24 that can cause us to be 'cold.' In verse three, David says, "Who may ascend the mountain of the Lord? Who may stand in his holy place?" Those are great coaching questions. How would you respond? What are your most significant challenges to stay 'hot?'

Next, in the following verse, David answers with these four challenges, "The one who has clean hands and a pure heart, who does not trust in an idol or swear by a false god." A suggestion now is to underline the four challenges to 'climbing the holy hill of the Lord' and take some time to let him speak to you about whether he's 'lost or found,' 'hot or cold' in your life.

As you're listening to what God is revealing to you, here are some thoughts about what we can do to develop habits to be 'hotter and hotter.' Consider doing some self-coaching around these questions:

- How will I practice the disciplines to nurture my relationship with God?
- How can I address busyness in my life?
- What step can I take toward better self-care?
- How can I prioritize my priorities?
- How can I draw a line to help make decisions for best things over good things?
- How can I intentionally walk being filled with the Holy Spirit?
- Who can I be accountable to with full transparency?

Making Room to Experience God

- What are the things that really matter, and how am I pursuing them?

When we conduct a two or three day training with church leaders; sometimes they chose to have a Discipleship Coach Training Retreat. Retreats provide an opportunity for leaders to get away, even if it's just a few miles from home. It's a chance to first 'unplug', in order to intentionally 'plug in' to God. Participants grow in relationship and return home revitalized with a clear vision for a discipleship plan that's relevant in their ministry. One valuable training piece is centered around worship; which includes the actual size of the Tabernacle being laid out proportionately. As the participants walk through the Tabernacle, they experience God's presence at the Ark of the Covenant in the Holy of Holies, the inner sanctuary of the Tabernacle where God dwelt.

> The 7 Disciplines of a disciple are more about our inward connection and encountering God than our outward activity. @nelsonroth

Worship is about experiencing God and is both a corporate and personal experience. It's giving worth (worship is derived from the Old English word "woerthship") to God when believers gather to praise him. Worship can also be an experience personally for the believer throughout the week. So, when we worship God either corporately or privately, we are proclaiming his worth and coming into his presence.

Entering In

How does connecting with God or experiencing him relate to the Old Testament Tabernacle and how can we as believers develop the habit of entering into the presence of God at any time? This is realized by understanding the transition that happened from the Old Testament to the New Testament, from the Old Covenant to the New Covenant, and from the Tabernacle worship and duties of the Priests of the Old Testament to the way believers have access to God through Jesus Christ our High Priest whose sacrifice makes this access possible today.

Hebrews chapters eight to ten give an account of this transition. In Hebrews 10:19-22, it says, "Therefore, brothers and sisters, since we have confidence to enter the Most Holy Place by the blood of Jesus, by a new and living way opened for us through the curtain, that is, his body, and since we have a great priest over the house of God, let us draw near to God with a sincere heart and with the full assurance that faith brings, having our hearts sprinkled to cleanse us from a guilty conscience and having our bodies washed with pure water."

Corporate worship is not driven by a particular style of music, but rather by experiencing God's remarkable presence and being impacted personally as we give worth to him. That personal impact leads to worship as a lifestyle, living a life that honors God and puts him in the center of everything.

Interestingly, the Tabernacle was at the center of the community life of Israel. It was the way they did 'city planning' when they pitched their tents. In the midst of the million or so Israelites was a central park or public place, the Tabernacle, where they gathered regularly. God being central was true logistically in how their camp was set up in the wilderness as well as spiritually in their lives. In this way, the people had a constant visual reminder of God's central position. Exodus 43:4-5, "The glory of the Lord entered the temple through the gate facing east. Then the Spirit lifted me up and brought me into the inner court, and the glory of the Lord filled the temple." Psalm 100:4, "Enter his gates with thanksgiving and his courts with praise; give thanks to him and praise his name."

God gave Israel a highly detailed way of coming into his presence through the outer court and inside the tabernacle. The Tabernacle and its contents illustrate the way Israel worshipped God and made sacrifices. It is a symbolic illustration of how Christians can experience and worship God today and on any day because of Jesus Christ, our High Priest.

Pause and Ponder

What can you do to experience God more often?
How can worship become more of a lifestyle for you?
In what way is God leading you to practice the 7 Disciplines to form new habits?

In *The Last Battle*, by C.S. Lewis, Jewel the Unicorn says, "I have come home at last! This is my real country! I belong here. This is the land I have been looking for all my life, though I never knew it till now...Come further up, come further in!" 3

Lewis' words, "come further up, come further in" inspired the lyrics of the song titled 'Enter In' by Jon Mohr, Steve Green, and Greg Nelson. Here's a great time to pause for a moment. As you read through these words and consider making room to experience God a holy habit, how will you respond?

Enter In 4

Nothing chills the heart of man
Like passing through death's gate
Yet to him who enters daily
Death's a glorious fate
Dearly beloved we are gathered here
To be a holy bride
And daily cross death's threshold
To the holy life inside

Chorus
Enter in, enter in
Surrender to the Spirit's call
To die and enter in
Enter in, find peace within
The holy life awaits you, enter in

The conflict still continues
Raging deep within my soul
My spirit wars against my flesh

In a struggle for control
My only hope is full surrender
So with each borrowed breath
I inhale the Spirit's will for me
To die a deeper death

Chorus
If mourners should lament
Let them weep for those alive
For only when my will is killed
Can my soul survive

In Luke 9:23-24, Then he (Jesus) said to them all: "Whoever wants to be my disciple must deny themselves and take up their cross daily and follow me. For whoever wants to save their life will lose it, but whoever loses their life for me will save it."

How will you respond to make room to experience God?

what leaders are saying...

I entered into a discipleship relationship with Nelson at a time when I felt God moving me to bring discipleship into my church; yet, realizing that I had never REALLY been discipled myself. My discipling relationship with Nelson unfolded organically; and, I soon realized it was not the presence of a lot of curriculum that led me into a deeper relationship with Christ. Rather, it was an intentional focus on the disciplines of a disciple and inviting God to open up my understanding and my connection to Him. This, coupled with my regular coaching conversations with Nelson, led to some amazing shifts in my heart and a deeper connection to the Almighty God

—Jeff Harmon
New Apostolic Church
Brilliance Within Coaching & Consulting
Parsippany, NJ

Becoming involved and discipled in the methods of the Relevant Discipleship Pathway has personally opened up the movement of the Holy Spirit, and put breath into how we are to live in relationship with God and all others in the world. With Christ as our guide, being given the grace and the space to rediscover and develop a lifestyle of loving God; discipleship becomes a way of life that is fully integrated, ongoing, relational, and absolutely authentic.

—Pastor Jenn Klein
Hamilton United Methodist Church
Hamilton, MO

10 multiplication

Our house sits on a piece of property that reaches to the finger of a 35-acre lake. The part of the lake, directly behind us is full of lily pads; and it's amazing how those lily pads multiply. Let's stop and think about the natural multiplication of lily pads for a minute. Imagine a pond the size of a baseball field. For the sake of an illustration, let's say we start with two lily pads in this pond and they multiply daily. On day one there are two, day two there are four, etc. Moving forward, if those lily pads keep multiplying till the pond is half filled with lily pads in three months, how long would it take to fill the other half of the pond?

> *What would a discipleship process that multiplies disciples integrated into the life of your church look like? @nelsonroth*

2 Timothy 2:2 says, "And the things you have heard me say in the presence of many witnesses entrust to reliable people who will also be qualified to teach

others." It sounds like Paul had the same idea in mind when he was writing to Timothy...multiply yourself. Did you figure out the answer to the lily pad question? If you said one more day, you're right! Wow, one more day for those lily pads to do what they had just done in the past three months. That's the exponential power of multiplication!

Disciple Maker

The Great Commission to 'make disciples' is not only about our personal commitment to follow Christ and grow as believers. The other part of Christ's plan is for us to become a disciple who becomes a disciple maker.

So how's that going in your life and ministry? An honest evaluation often reveals, that becoming a disciple maker has as many challenges as our personal journey of being a disciple. In this chapter, we will consider the challenges of multiplication or better yet, let's refer to it as evangelism. What might happen if we connected discipleship and evangelism and started to see these two words more like twins or two sides of the same coin, instead of distant cousins?

Let's first address thoughts or perceptions we might have about evangelism. What is the first thought that comes to your mind when you hear the word evangelism? You may want to pause right here and think about that question before you continue to read.

The dictionary says, evangelism is the spreading of the Christian Gospel by public preaching or personal witness. What comes to your mind? What can be learned, or depending on your perception, what might you need to unlearn?

My first experience with evangelism was handing out tracts and knocking on doors of people I didn't know. I was a young follower and on staff at a church. I wanted to be faithful to what I was being asked to do; however, I confess for me personally it was a struggle. Tuesday nights at our church were a challenge for me because this was the night the faithful gathered at the church to go out with cards that had names and addresses assigned for visitation. Being completely honest, each time I rang a doorbell, I prayed no one would be at home. I was always glad when Tuesday nights were over because I didn't have to think about evangelism again until the next week. How about you? What's your perception around evangelism?

I also remember a time, just before a revival at our church, when we were challenged to hand out five tracts a day for the week leading up to the revival. We were encouraged to put five tracts in our shirt pocket at the start of the day and not come home that night until we had handed out all five tracts. Can I be honest again? Most nights, I remember stopping at a gas station on the way home, going to the restroom and putting all five tracts on the sink. It was the way I relieved my guilt so I could go back home that evening. So, what's your experience around evangelism?

Evangelism is one of the 7 Disciplines on the Relevant Discipleship Pathway™. The short description of Evangelism is cultivating intentional friendships with not-yet believers. The Acts and Revelation scripture references for the discipline of Evangelism are:

- The early church was "...enjoying the favor of all the people. And the Lord added to their number daily those who were being saved." (Acts 2:47)
- The reference to the church at Laodecia says, the church was "lukewarm." They were self-sufficient and inward focused. (Revelation 3:16)

Bright Lights

How did the early church in Acts practice or walk out evangelism? The answer is they were "enjoying the favor of all the people." The 'all the people' is a reference to the people in Jerusalem who were not-yet believers. This verse is telling us the believers were letting their lights shine so bright, they were attractive to those who were not-yet believers, so much so, they wanted what the believers had. Then the verse goes on to say, "the Lord added to their number daily those who were being saved." So, what might churches look like if this were equally true today?

> Disciples making disciples, a transformational process of multiplying devoted followers of Christ. That's the goal of Relevant Discipleship. @nelsonroth

Around the topic of evangelism, Joe Aldridge writes in his book, *Lifestyle Evangelism*, "The best argument for Christianity is Christians: their joy, their certainty, their completeness. But the strongest argument against Christianity is also Christians — when they are somber and joyless, when they are self-righteous and smug in complacent consecration, when they are narrow and repressive, then Christianity dies a thousand deaths." [1]

Another important concept that I have learned is the significance of a balance between what I call 'presence' and 'proclamation' when it comes to evangelism. Through genuine friendship, from our friends' perspective, we earn the right to speak into their lives. Evangelism begins with 'presence' and at the right time, 'proclamation.' All the time depending on God to do his work in his timing.

John confirms this in John 6:44 when he wrote the words of Jesus saying, "No one can come to me unless the Father who sent me draws them, and I will raise them up at the last day." We also read in John 3:1-8 about the new birth experience of Nicodemus. Every believer who desires to be the hands, feet, and mouth of Jesus must understand what it says in verse eight. "The wind blows wherever it pleases. You hear its sound, but you cannot tell where it comes from or where it is going. So it is with everyone born of the Spirit." No human being can make this happen. Our evangelism efforts must cooperate with the Spirit of the living God. In every situation, we must depend upon the Holy Spirit to present opportunities to minister the truth and life of Jesus.

Peter also speaks about our 'presence' in 1 Peter 3:15, "But in your hearts revere Christ as Lord. Always be prepared to give an answer to everyone who asks you to give the reason for the hope that you have. But do this with gentleness and respect." So, we let our light shine. Then, a friend who is a not-yet believer is curious and "asks you to give the reason for the hope that you have." How close does that sound to the early church? "...enjoying the favor of all the people. And the Lord added to their number daily those who were being saved."

There are times when we speak or proclaim. It's a chance to share our story of conversion and the difference that Christ has made in our lives. Paul speaks of this in Romans 10:14, "How, then, can they call on the one they have not believed in? And how can they believe in the one of whom they have not heard? And how can they hear without someone preaching to them?" Then in verse seventeen, "Consequently, faith comes from hearing the message, and the message is heard through the word about Christ."

Pause and Ponder

How have your evangelism experiences shaped you?
What would help you to move forward as
a disciple maker?

After my earlier experiences of handing out tracts and knocking on doors, you might say, my view of evangelism was rocked when I heard about "friendship evangelism." It seems unthinkable to me now that I thought this was such a radical approach. When in fact, it only makes sense that we have to take the time to make friends first before we can begin to share about Christ.

"What? Take the time to make friends?" At first, I resisted this concept with the justification that, "Jesus is coming back and making this important decision is urgent for people!" However, the book, *Lifestyle Evangelism*, quoted earlier helped shift my paradigm and broke ground for this new approach to evangelism.

Also, during this transition process, I picked up this slogan from somewhere that had an impact on me ... "People don't care how much you know until they know how much you care." Moving forward to today, I've come to see that relationships that are genuine with others are essential in this matter of introducing others to God's love and his redemption provided through his Son, Jesus Christ.

> If evangelism is pre-conversion discipleship, how are you engaging with not-yet believers? @nelsonroth

Multiplication Through Discipleship Evangelism

So, now I'm wondering, does the term discipleship evangelism begin to make sense? It's the idea of discipling people to Jesus and then on to maturity. To explore this idea of discipleship evangelism, I want us to see with a fresh perspective how Jesus conducted himself during his three years of ministry. And, I also want to explore the Celtic Way of evangelism. Are you familiar with St. Patrick? Before we consider methods of Jesus and St. Patrick, here's a great quote about discipleship evangelism from Aubrey Malphurs. "Jesus was clear about his intentions for his church...to move people along a maturity or disciple-making continuum from Pre Birth (unbelief) to the New Birth (belief) and then to Maturity." [2] Malphurs presents the same idea of discipling people to Jesus as part of the disciple-making process.

As we consider Jesus' method of evangelism or multiplication and the idea of discipleship evangelism, the Relevant Discipleship Pathway™ diagram, found in the Appendix on page 178, will be helpful. The following four points, on the way into the center of the pathway, can help us see Jesus' method of evangelism. Along the way during Jesus' ministry, curiosity about Jesus led to the conversion of many.

> First, Jesus put out the call to "come and see." This call is pre-conversion discipleship. It is for us, engaging culture intentionally through authentic relationship and at the right time, having spiritual conversations with not-yet believers. ['make disciples' as you're going and sharing the Gospel, Matthew 28:19]

> Next, Jesus said, "come follow me." Here is where a person makes the conscious decision to believe and begin to follow. This call is where a one-to-one discipleship experience is vital for

growth and transformation. ['make disciples' by baptizing them, Matthew 28:19]

Then, Jesus said, "come and be with me." This is about small group community. Forming small missional groups that learn, serve together, and live life on mission. Not-yet believers are invited to this setting, and the small group becomes a place for evangelism. Remember, the Great Commission is 'plural' grammatically. It wasn't given to only me, it was given to all of us. ['make disciples' by teaching them to obey, Matthew 28:20]

Then in the center, it's the "abide in me" or, experiencing God when gathered together for weekend worship and celebration. Small groups in a church gather on weekends to celebrate what God has been doing throughout the week.

Pause and Ponder

What are your thoughts on the word evangelism?
How much sense is the idea of discipleship
evangelism making to you?
What are you learning?
What are you unlearning?

Belonging Then Believing

We've seen Jesus' method by starting with the invitation to "come and see." Now, let's look at what we can learn from St. Patrick and what George Hunter calls the Celtic Way. In his book, *The Celtic Way of Evangelism: How Christianity Can Reach the West...Again*, he says, "There is no shortcut to understanding the people. When you understand the people, you often know what to say and do and how. When the people know that the Christians understand them, they infer that maybe Christianity's High God understands them too." [3]

In his book, Hunter points out the difference between what he calls the Roman Way and the Celtic Way of evangelism. Bottom line, Hunter informs us that Patrick was concerned first about the people and valued relationships. He calls it 'belonging'...helping people feel like they belong so that they might believe. Hunter declares the Roman Way, or the Western Way evangelizes the direct opposite of the Celtic Way. We'll talk more about that in a few minutes, but first, let's get to know St. Patrick.

Patrick lived in Britain, during the fifth century, but was captured as a teenager by pirates and enslaved in Ireland. He was a slave cattle-herder for six years. In his trials, Patrick found God. After six years, he escaped and pursued theological training in Britain. Thirty years later, Patrick returned as a missionary to Ireland. A considerable motivation for his missionary work was he knew the people of Ireland. And because of that, God gave him a love and passion for sharing Jesus Christ to them! It's recorded that in twenty-nine years of ministry, over 120,000 baptisms were performed and over 300 churches were started. Patrick's ministry was separate from the Roman Catholic Church. Four centuries later the Catholic Church adopted him in and declared him Saint Patrick in the 9th Century.

What's the difference between the Celtic Way and the Roman Way? The Roman Way presents the Gospel first, then asks for a decision, and then brings the new convert into the fellowship. Patrick did it this way...fellowship or genuinely giving the not-yet believer the sense of belonging, then conversations and ministry, followed by confession and belief.

What did Patrick do right? Patrick's Celtic Christianity provides a model for evangelism through individual example and community. Here are some points acquired from Hunter's book to consider as a disciple maker:

- A distinctive was intentional solitude, drawing away from the clan for time alone with the Creator. A focus on being a disciple.
- Each believer was to have a companion in the journey, an *anamchara* (or "soul friend") who would be not a spiritual superior but a friend and peer who could nurture a safe place for transparency, vulnerability, accountability, support, and challenge.

- The next element of this community was a mentor-led small group of fellow believers who would join in study and service.
- The experience expanded to ordinary, everyday life: meals, labor, biblical teaching, prayer, and worship.
- The above aspects combined to compel each member of the community to interact with pre-Christians who had not yet understood the promise of the Gospel.

Hunter refers to how the Celts evangelized by first creating communities which developed into a disciplined spirituality creating an effective witness of Christ in the world. It's an incredible story. Celtic Christianity flourished among the people of Ireland during the Middle Ages. It was one of the most successful evangelistic branches of the church in history. The Celtic church converted Ireland from paganism to Christianity in a remarkably short period and then sent missionaries throughout Europe.

If as Hunter says, our Roman Way is the inversion of the Celtic Way, what shifts would be necessary for us to multiply? What do we need to change about our approach to evangelism? What will be the challenges of making those changes?

What would be your plan for taking a Celtic approach? Here is a review of the Celtic Way:

1. The potential believer is first offered fellowship and hospitality.

2. Then, fellowship and hospitality lead to the opportunity for service and authentic spiritual conversations.
3. After this, connection and commitment are built and trusted. The prospective Christian may choose belief and conversion based on the reality of the relationship, leading to full inclusion in the community.

Jesus' practice was to call those who were excluded. In the story about the call of Matthew in Luke 5:27-32, Jesus went out and saw a tax collector by the name of Levi sitting at his tax booth. "Follow me," Jesus said to him...the Pharisees and the teachers questioning said, 'Why do you eat and drink with tax collectors and sinners?' Jesus answered them, 'It is not the healthy who need a doctor, but the sick. I have not come to call the righteous, but sinners to repentance.'"

> *Where did Jesus go to connect with people? Out of 120 connections recorded in the New Testament, ten or so were in the temple or synagogue, 100+ were daily life encounters.*
> *@nelsonroth*

Let me begin to wrap up this chapter by listing each of the five times we find the Great Commission in the New Testament. Pause after reading each one and listen to how God may be speaking to you about multiplication and making disciples.

Then Jesus came to them and said, 'All authority in heaven and on earth has been given to me. Therefore go and make disciples of all nations, baptizing them in the name of the Father and of the Son and of the Holy Spirit, and teaching them to obey everything I have commanded you. And surely I am with you always, to the very end of the age.' (Matthew 28:18-20)

He said to them, 'Go into all the world and preach the Gospel to all creation...' (Mark 16:15)

He told them, 'This is what is written: The Messiah will suffer and rise from the dead on the third day, and repentance for the forgiveness of sins will be preached in his name to all nations, beginning at Jerusalem.' (Luke 24:46-47)

Again Jesus said, 'Peace be with you! As the Father has sent me, I am sending you.' And with that he breathed on them and said, 'Receive the Holy Spirit.' (John 20:21-22)

'But you will receive power when the Holy Spirit comes on you; and you will be my witnesses in Jerusalem, and in all Judea and Samaria, and to the ends of the earth.' (Acts 1:8)

From the beginning of time to present time, God's plan has been about multiplication. Moving forward, how will you "be fruitful and increase in number" (Genesis 1:28)?

Along with reading the history of St. Patrick, I've been listening to Celtic music. I love the melodies and the instruments. Listening causes me to both stand up and shout; and, bow down and worship. I close this chapter and the book with the words to one of the Celtic songs I've listened to over and over. May these words inspire you. Inspiration or motivation is the 'why' we do what we do. Around discipleship and all you've hopefully gleaned and put into practice from this book, my prayer is for you and for me that the words of this song will be motivation to continue on with what really matters in this life.

"When It's All Been Said And Done" by Robin Mark [4]

When it's all been said and done
There is just one thing that matters
Did I do my best to live for truth?
Did I live my life for you?

When it's all been said and done
All my treasures will mean nothing
Only what I've done for love's reward

Will stand the test of time

Lord, your mercy is so great
That you look beyond our weakness
And find purest gold in miry clay
Making sinners into saints.

And I will always sing your praise
Here on earth and ever after
For you've shown me Heaven's my true home
When it's all been said and done
You're my life when life is gone…

what leaders are saying…

I am so excited about this discipleship process multiplying our efforts as a church to help people find and follow Christ. The opportunity to exponentially grow discipleship within the church is outstanding. This process will help us leverage next steps for everyone, whether they haven't committed their life to Christ yet or have been following him for many years.

—Kevin Beachy, Lead Pastor
Gulf Coast Church
Long Beach, MS

Experiencing Relevant Discipleship has taught me a process to multiply discipleship. I will always be thankful to God for Relevant Ministry and their sincere dedication to helping me and my church.

—Philip McMurrin
Pastor, Concord United Methodist Church
Brooksville, KY
Chaplain, Hospice of Hope
Maysville, KY

What I found in the Relevant Discipleship Pathway is a discipleship pathway that actually has potential for making and multiplying disciples. An added bonus is spending time focusing on the 7 disciplines with my Relevant Discipleship Coach that has energized and deepened my own relationship with God.

—Phyllis Riney, D. Min., PCC
Discipleship Coach
Texas Conference UMC
Houston, TX

what's next

Relevant Discipleship™ and Coach Training

Relevant Ministry trains and helps leaders implement the tried and proven pathway process of discipleship with a coaching approach in churches in the United States and around the world. Our flagship course is Level 401 Certificate in Discipleship Coaching. Relevant Ministry trains at all 4 Training Levels. As leaders are trained to be Discipleship Overseers and Relevant Discipleship Coaches they train at various levels as well. Where you are currently on the Relevant Discipleship Pathway™ will determine your next steps for training.

4 Training Level Descriptions

1. Believers

101 Train the Discipler™ Workshop #1 (3 hrs)
Practical instruction for a lifelong journey of following Jesus Christ as a disciple. Jesus' call to fishermen at the Sea of Galilee was to first, "Follow me..." Matthew 4:19a

102 Train the Discipler™ Workshop #2 (3 hrs)
Transformation and multiplication are the central themes. As believers continue to 'grow' they 'go'

and Jesus will do his part to "make you fishers of men." Matthew 4:19b

2. Culture Changers

201 Introduction to Relevant Discipleship Pathway™ (6 hrs)

A biblical perspective of the chronological stages of Jesus' ministry; future leaders of groups/classes learn a life-changing discipleship pathway.

202 Introduction to Coaching Techniques (4 hrs)

Future leaders of groups/classes develop coaching techniques. You will observe and practice one-to-one and group discipleship coaching. The Nehemiah Response Coaching Model™ will be your guide for discipleship coaching conversations.

301 Discipleship Coaching (12 hrs)

Pastors and leaders of groups/classes who desire to develop a transformational, multiplying discipleship culture will look at discipleship from a biblical perspective and develop a personal ministry philosophy around discipleship. Participants will discover the Relevant Discipleship Pathway™ along with a coaching approach that will jumpstart an intentional discipleship movement that transforms believers and multiplies disciples.

302 Coach Training for Discipleship (8 hrs)

A foundational course for coach training designed to equip pastors and leaders of groups/classes with basic coaching skills in both one-to-one and group settings. Participants will:

- Recognize the difference between coaching and counseling, consulting, and mentoring
- Develop fundamental coaching skills
- Receive a combination of coaching theory and practice
- Observe and practice coaching
- Learn the Nehemiah Response Coaching Model™

3. Discipleship Overseers

401 Certificate in Discipleship Coaching (24 hrs)

An interactive course for pastors, church leaders, and leaders of missional communities aspiring to develop a transformational, multiplying discipleship culture within their ministry context. Leaders will develop a plan along with essential skills to confidently become a Discipleship Overseer in their church.

4. Relevant Discipleship Coaches

402 Professional Coach Training for Discipleship (16 hrs)

Are you ready to take your first step toward getting certified as a Christian discipleship coach?

Whether your goal is advancing in your coaching skills or becoming a professional certified coach with an ICF ACC credential this training will meet your expectations.

403 Professional Coach Training for Discipleship (24 hrs)

The twenty-four hours of training will not only take your coaching skills to a next level it will also complete the forty hours of required Professional Coach Training by the ICF. Along with the twenty-four hours of the Certificate in Discipleship Coaching, you will have the required sixty-four hours for an ACC credential.

Mentor Coaching with a Discipleship Focus (10 hrs)

Relevant Ministry provides the ten hours of Mentor Coaching required by the ICF following your sixty-four hours of Professional Coach Training.

The **Relevant Discipleship Network™** is a collective of like-minded leaders who connect for mutual encouragement and training around discipleship.

For the current training schedule, visit www.relevantministry.org/training.

appendix

Three Concentric Circles of Relevant Discipleship™
The 7 Disciplines of a disciple and the 3Rs

The 7 Disciplines of a disciple come from the DNA of the New Testament church found in Acts 2:42-47 and also from the seven churches of Revelation.

The 3Rs come directly from the Greatest Commandment and the Great Commission of the New Testament. These core values are vital to Relevant Discipleship™ and are evidences of spiritual health in the life and ministry of a disciple; along with the practice of the 7 Disciplines, Christ followers and their churches are transformed.

Suggested Reading:
Relevant Discipleship™ Resource Manual: resources for practicing the disciplines of a disciple

Relevant Discipleship Pathway™

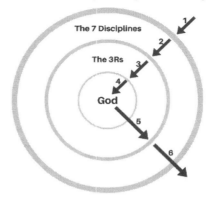

The inward and outward journey of the Relevant Discipleship Pathway™

The 7 Disciplines of a disciple flow inward, and when practiced, makes room for us to experience God. The Pathway then flows outward from the center bringing transformation in our lives around the 3Rs - Relational, Responsive, Reveals Christ.

Here is the timeline of how Jesus interacted with disciples:
1. *"Come and see"* - John 1:35-46 (4-5 months)
2. *"Come, follow me"* - Mark 1:16-20 (10-11 months)
3. *"He appointed twelve that they might be with him"* - Mark 3:13-14 (20 months)
4. *"Remain / Abide in me and I in you"* - John 15:5-8 (final instructions before the cross)
5. *"Everyone ... fully trained will be like their teacher"* - Luke 6:40 (transformation, 2 years)
6. *"Let your light shine before others"* - Matthew 5:14-16 (2 years)

Suggested Reading:
Relevant Discipleship™ Resource Manual: resources for practicing the disciplines of a disciple

Nehemiah Response Coaching Model™

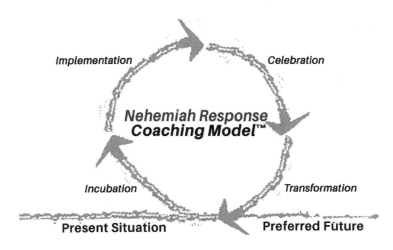

The Nehemiah Response Coaching Model™ is a biblical, transitional process for revitalization and transformation. The model helps guide the conversation during your one-to-one discipleship sessions

The Nehemiah Response Coaching Model™ captures responses of Nehemiah and will help to develop a custom solution to get from where your are (Present Situation) to where you want to go (Preferred Future).

The metaphor for the graphic has two parts, a circle and a line - a circle rolling forward along a line to your Preferred Future from your Present Situation. The four stages of the circle help with traction to move forward.

Suggested Reading:
Nehemiah Response: a coaching model, Nelson and Pam Roth

Discipleship Evangelism and the Relevant Discipleship Pathway™

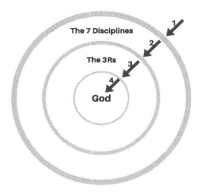

Discipleship evangelism is to disciple people to Jesus and on to maturity.
@nelsonroth

Each of the four stages, into the center, help us see Jesus' method of evangelism.

1. **Pre-conversion discipleship**
    "Come and see"
    Intentionally engaging culture through authentic relationships and spiritual conversations.

2. **Transforming discipleship**
    "Come follow me"
    A person makes the conscious decision to believe and begin to follow. One-to-one

discipleship is vital for growth and transformation.

3. **Small group community**
   "Come be with me"
   Living life on mission - learning and serving together. Not-yet believers are invited to this setting, and the small group becomes a place for evangelism.

4. **Gathering for worship and celebration**
   "Abide in me"
   Weekend celebration of God's working and experiencing him throughout the week.

Suggested Reading:
Relevant Discipleship™ Resource Manual: resources for practicing the disciplines of a disciple

notes

Introduction
1. Aubrey Malphurs, Strategic Disciple Making: A Practical Tool for Successful Ministry, page 13

Chapter 1 What is Discipleship
1. Vine's Expository Dictionary of New Testament Words, disciple, Noun, mathetes
2. Dallas Willard, Renovation of the Heart:Putting On the Character of Christ, page 19
3. Alan Hirsch, The Forgotten Ways: Reactivating Apostolic Movements, page 11
4. George Barna, Growing True Disciples: New Strategies for Producing Genuine Followers of Christ, page 2

Chapter 2 What to Do
1. Alexander Balmain Bruce, The Training of the Twelve: Timeless Principles for Leadership Development, page 10

Chapter 3 What to Say

1. J. Val Hasting, *The Next Great Awakening: How to Empower God's People with a Coach Approach to Ministry*, page 21

Chapter 4 First Things First

1. Dietrich Bonhoeffer, *The Cost of Discipleship*, pages 35-36
2. Theodore Monod, *None of Self and All of Thee*, published 1875

Chapter 5 Practicing the 7 Disciplines

1. Richard J. Foster, *Celebration of Discipline: The Path to Spiritual Growth*, page 7
2. *Longing for God: Seven Paths of Christian Devotion*, Foster and Beebe, page 13

Chapter 6 The Outcome, Ongoing Transformation

1. St. Richard of Chichester, *Day by Day*, https://en.wikipedia.org/wiki/Richard_of_Chichester
2. Dietrich Bonhoeffer, *The Cost of Discipleship*, page 99
3. Dallas Willard, *Renovation of the Heart: Putting On the Character of Christ*, from Introduction
4. Nelson and Pam Roth, *Nehemiah Response: a coaching model*, page 146
5. Jerry Bridges, *The Pursuit of Holiness*, page 77

Chapter 7 The Holy Spirit

1. Martyn Lloyd-Jones, *Joy Unspeakable, Power and Renewal in the Holy Spirit*, page 17

2. Martyn Lloyd-Jones, *Joy Unspeakable, Power and Renewal in the Holy Spirit*, page 17-18

3. Andrew Murray, *Absolute Surrender*, page 2

Chapter 8 Resources to Get Started

1. Greg Ogden, *Transforming Discipleship*, page 43

Chapter 9 Making Room to Experience God

1. *The Practice of the Presence of God*, by Brother Lawrence, Ninth Letter, p. 48

2. Henri Nouwan, *From Solitude to Community to Ministry*, http://www.christianitytoday.com/pastors/1995/spring/5l280.html

3. *The Last Battle*, C.S. Lewis, page 161

4. *Enter In, Words and Music by Jon Mohr*, Steve Green and Greg Nelson, Copyright 1986 Jonathan Mark Music/Birdwing Music

Chapter 10 Multiplication

1. Joseph Aldridge, *Lifestyle Evangelism, learning to open your life to those around you*, page 21

2. Aubrey Malphurs, *Strategic Disciple Making: A Practical Tool for Successful Ministry*, page 19

3. George Hunter, *The Celtic Way of Evangelism: How Christianity Can Reach the West...Again*, page 8

4. Robin Mark, *When It's All Been Said And Done, from the album Revival In Belfast*. Arranged by Dan Galbraith/David Shipps

bibliography

David Augsburger, *Dissident Discipleship: A Spirituality of Self-Surrender, Love of God, and Love of Neighbor*

George Barna, *Growing True Disciples: New Strategies for Producing Genuine Followers of Christ*

Dietrich Bonhoeffer, *The Cost of Discipleship*

Mike Breen and Steve Cockram, *Building a Discipleship Culture: how to release a missional movement by discipling people like Jesus did*

Jerry Bridges, *The Pursuit of Holiness*

A.B. Bruce, *The Training of the Twelve: timeless principles for leadership development*

Robert Coleman, *The Master Plan of Evangelism*

Leroy Eims, *The Lost Art of Disciple Making*

Richard Foster, *Celebration of Discipline: The Path to Spiritual Growth*

Richard Foster and Gayle Beebe, *Longing for God: Seven Paths of Christian Devotion*

Alan Hirsch, *The Forgotten Ways: Reactivating Apostolic Movements*

Alan Hirsch and Debra Hirsch, *Untamed: Reactivating a Missional Form of Discipleship*

Bill Hull, *The Complete Book of Discipleship: on Being and Making Followers of Christ*

George Hunter, *The Celtic Way of Evangelism: How Christianity Can Reach the West...Again*

Robert E. Logan, *The Discipleship Difference: Making Disciples While Growing As Disciples*

Robert E. Logan, *The Missional Journey: multiplying disciples and churches that transform the world*

Gordon MacDonald, *Ordering Your Private World*

Aubrey Malphurs, *Strategic Disciple Making: A Practical Tool for Successful Ministry*

Phil Maynard, *Membership to Discipleship: Growing Mature Disciples Who Make Disciples*

Dennis McCallum and Jessica Lowery, *Organic Discipleship: Mentoring Others into Spiritual Maturity and Leadership*

Henri Nouwen, *The Way of the Heart: Connecting with God Through Prayer, Wisdom, and Silence*

Henri Nouwen, *A Spirituality of Living*

Greg Ogden, *Transforming Discipleship: Making Disciples a Few at a Time*

J.I. Packer, *Knowing God*

Jim Putman and Bobby Harrington, *Discipleship Shift: Five Steps That Help Your Church to Make Disciples Who Make Disciples*

Francis A. Schaeffer, *The Mark of a Christian*

Ray Stedman, *Authentic Christianity: How Lutheran Theology Speaks to a Postmodern World*

John Stott, *The Radical Disciple: Some Neglected Aspects of Our Calling*

Leonard Sweet, *I Am a Follower: The Way, Truth, and Life of Following Jesus*

Dallas Willard, *Renovation of the Heart: Putting on the Character of Christ*

Dallas Willard, *The Spirit of the Disciplines: Understanding How God Changes Lives*

Dallas Willard, *The Great Omission: Reclaiming Jesus's Essential Teachings on Discipleship*

glossary

Important Relevant Discipleship™ terms and concepts

3Rs

The 3Rs come directly from the Greatest Commandment and the Great Commission of the New Testament. These core values are vital in the discipleship process and are evidences of spiritual health in life and ministry. Transformation is experienced around the 3Rs...(1) relationship with God, (2) responding to others and (3) revealing Christ.

See Chapter 2: subheading, Core Aspects of Discipleship (page 40)
See Chapter 6: subheading, Transformed Around the 3Rs (page 93)

7 Disciplines

The 7 Disciplines of a disciple come from the DNA of the New Testament church found in Acts 2:42-47 and also from the seven churches of Revelation. The 7 Disciplines are:

- Worship
- Prayer
- Word
- Ministry

- Discipleship
- Community
- Evangelism

See Chapter 2: subheading, Core Aspects of Discipleship (page 40)
See Chapter 5: subheading, The 7 Disciplines (page 78)
See Chapter 5: subheading, The Church in The Last Days (page 82)
See Chapter 5: subheading, How to Practice the 7 Disciplines (page 85)

Action and Accountability

Action and Accountability is one of the three coaching techniques used in discipleship coaching. This particular technique helps the person put a plan together and commit to follow through.

See Chapter 3: subheading, Action and Accountability (page 58)

Being a disciple

"Come, follow me, and I will send you out to fish for people" (Matthew 4:19). Jesus' first request was to 'follow' and then 'fish.' A disciple is a learner and a follower.

See Chapter 1: subheading, Being and Making (page 29)
See Chapter 8: subheading, Lifelong Journey: Experiencing the Pathway (page 131)

Coaching

Here are three definitions of coaching, two from professional coaches and the other from the International Coach Federation:

Coaching is partnering with clients in a thought-provoking and creative process that inspires them to maximize their personal and professional potential. (International Coach Federation)

As a coach, I help people get the results they want by bringing out the best in them in a developmental or discovery-based process. (J. Val Hastings – Coaching4Clergy)

Coaching is the process of coming alongside a person to help them discover God's agenda for their life and ministry, and then cooperating with the Holy Spirit to see that agenda become a reality. (Bob Logan, *Coaching 101 Handbook*)

See Chapter 3, What To Say (page 51)

Coaching Approach

What's unique about Relevant Discipleship™ is the coaching approach! With a coaching approach to discipleship, you can relax and enjoy incredible spiritual conversations with others. Disciple makers utilizing the coaching approach ask powerful questions rather than tell, are good listeners, and provide accountability to the person while they are making discovery and creating actions steps. For a more thorough and comprehensive look at the coaching approach, read *Nehemiah Response: a coaching model.*

See Chapter 3: subheading, Discipleship Coaching (page 52)

Coaching Techniques

Disciple makers utilizing the coaching approach (1) ask powerful questions rather than tell, (2) are good listeners, and (3) provide accountability to the person while they are making discovery and creating actions steps. These coaching techniques, when applied with the discipleship pathway, result in meaningful and transformational changes in a person's life.

See Chapter 3: subheading, Three Coaching Techniques (54)

Deep Listening

Deep Listening is about the disciple maker being inquisitive. To be inquisitive, you need to be fully present and intently listen. Listening doesn't come naturally and takes practice. Often our normal response is to tell or to fix the situation.
See Chapter 3: subheading, Deep Listening (page 57)

Disciple

A disciple is a learner and a follower who commits to a lifetime of knowing Christ, growing in Christ, serving Christ, and sharing Christ with the world.
See Chapter 1: subheading, Defining Discipleship (page 31)
See Chapter 4: subheading, Christian or Disciple (page 65)

Discipleship Evangelism

Discipleship evangelism is the idea of discipling people to Jesus and then on to maturity.
See Chapter 10: subheading, Multiplication Through Discipleship Evangelism (page 159)

Discipler

As a discipler you contextualize discipleship and consider where the disciplee is at the time with the coaching approach. Relevant Discipleship™ is a relational process where two people, a discipler and a disciplee, commit to meet one-to-one; welcoming the Holy Spirit to guide in each session.
See Chapter 5: subheading, How to Practice the 7 Disciplines (page 85)

Discipleship Sessions

Relevant Discipleship™ is a continuous journey of a series of six-month discipleship sessions where two people meet

practicing the 7 Disciplines of a disciple in an effort to make room to experience God allowing the indwelling Holy Spirit to transform us to be more like Christ.
See Chapter 8: subheading, Content: Articles, Coaching Tools, and Lessons (page 129)

Discipleship Coaching
Coaching is the 'secret sauce' to Relevant Discipleship™. Discipleship Coaching takes discipleship up a notch.
See Chapter 3: subheading, Discipleship Coaching (page 52)

Evangelism
Evangelism is a balance between what can be called 'presence' and 'proclamation.' Through genuine friendship, from our friends' perspective, we earn the right to speak into their lives.
See Chapter 10: subheading, Bright Lights (page 156)

Framework
The framework of the pathway is the system or skeletal structure that supports an ongoing, growing spiritual life.
See Chapter 8: subheading, Process (page 128)

Holy Spirit
The Holy Spirit was the power of the original disciples of Christ. As Christ's disciples today our source of power is the same. Being and making disciples requires the Spirit's power.
See Chapter 7: subheading, Promise of the Spirit (page 112)

Intentional
As we live the life of a disciple, we're to be deliberate about our practice of the disciplines. The outcome of

intentionality like this is experiencing God at work and then choosing to join him in that work.
See Chapter 5: subheading, Intentionality (page 77)

Making disciples
Matthew 28:19, "Therefore go and make disciples..." The Great Commission to 'make disciples' is not only about our personal commitment to follow Christ and grow as believers; part of Christ's plan is for us to become a disciple who becomes a disciple maker.
See Chapter 10: subheading, Disciple Maker (page 154)

Multiply
Paul instructs Timothy to multiply himself in 2 Timothy 2:2, "And the things you have heard me say in the presence of many witnesses entrust to reliable people who will also be qualified to teach others." From the beginning of time to present time, God's plan has been about multiplication, "be fruitful and increase in number" Genesis 1:28.
See Chapter 10, Multiplication (page 153)

Nehemiah Response Coaching Model™
The Nehemiah Response Coaching Model™ is a tool to help with knowing 'what to say.' The Nehemiah Response Coaching Model™ is a biblical, transformational process for revitalization and change. The model captures responses of Nehemiah and will help you develop a custom solution to get from where you are (Present Situation) to where you want to go (Preferred Future). The Nehemiah Response Coaching Model™ provides a reproducible and repeatable strategic process for positive change in life and ministry.
See Appendix, Nehemiah Response Coaching Model™ (page 177)

One-to-One
We use the term one-to-one, rather than one-on-one. One-on-one is more of an athletic term suggesting competitiveness. One-to-one is more relational. Discipleship also happens in other settings like classes and groups. To add one-to-one discipleship coaching takes discipleship to deeper levels.
See Chapter 8: subheading, One-to-One (page 134)

Powerful Questions
Powerful questions are open-ended; leaving room for a person to respond with answers that could set them on course for a plan and purpose to grow spiritually. Most often, people ask closed-ended questions, only allowing for 'yes' or 'no' answers; or at best, a short statement.
See Chapter 3: subheading, Powerful Questions (page 54)

Practice of the Disciplines
Practicing a discipline a certain way is not about doing the discipline so we can check it off; rather, it's about practicing the discipline in order to make room to know and experience God. When we practice the 7 Disciplines, we form new habits.
See Chapter 5: subheading, How to Practice the 7 Disciplines (page 85)
See Chapter 5: subheading, Forming New Habits (page 87)
See Chapter 9: subheading, Practice of the Presence (page 138)

Relevant Discipleship Pathway™
The Relevant Discipleship Pathway™ is a framework for intentional transformation and multiplication. While you're experiencing discipleship, the Relevant Discipleship Pathway™ is a tool to help with knowing 'what to do.'

The inspiration for the pathway comes from the chronological stages of Jesus' ministry.

Relevant Ministry, Inc.
Relevant Ministry is a biblically-based, interdenominational ministry that equips leaders and empowers individuals to minister relevantly in healthy and thriving churches.

Salvation
Salvation is knowing and following Jesus Christ. John 10:27-28, "My sheep listen to my voice; I know them, and they follow me. I give them eternal life..." Salvation is necessary because of sin. Salvation is required because of the righteousness of God. God is a Holy God and must punish sin. God is also a God of love and has provided a way of salvation through Jesus Christ. Salvation is the good news of the Gospel!
See Chapter 4: subheading, Knowing Christ (page 64)

Transformation
Transformation begins and continues with the partnership of the Holy Spirit. The outcome of practicing the 7 Disciplines is godliness. "Do not conform to the pattern of this world, but be transformed by the renewing of your mind. Then you will be able to test and approve what God's will is—his good, pleasing and perfect will" (Romans 12:2).
See Chapter 6: subheading, Transformed Around the 3Rs (page 93)

Way of Life
Discipleship is a lifelong journey. It's not a curriculum to complete. It's a way of life for the rest of your life. Once you have experienced the pathway for the initial six-month

period, what's next? We're to continue, because the discipleship pathway is a continual process, a way of life.

See Introduction (page 25)
See Chapter 2: subheading, A Way of Life for the Rest of Your Life (page 47)

resources for Relevant DiscipleshipTM

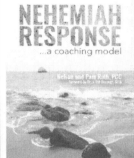

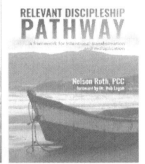

Relevant Discipleship Resource Manual: resources for practicing the disciplines of a disciple, Relevant Ministry

Nehemiah Response: a coaching model, Nelson and Pam Roth

Relevant Discipleship Pathway: a framework for intentional transformation that multiplies, Nelson Roth

How to use these resources:

One-to-One Discipleship Coaching
Relevant DiscipleshipTM is a relational process where two people commit to meet one-to-one; welcoming the Holy Spirit to guide in each session. There is a suggested six-month period, meeting every three

weeks intentionally around the 7 Disciplines of a disciple, using the articles and coaching tools in the *Relevant Discipleship™ Resource Manual.* The one-to-one discipleship sessions are reinforced within the context of a small group or class using the lessons in the *Relevant Discipleship™ Resource Manual* when your group or class is gathered.

Small Groups or Sunday School Classes:
Consider using the twelve lessons of the *Relevant Discipleship™ Resource Manual* to reinforce the one-to-one discipleship sessions of your group or class members. Also consider an eleven-week book study in your group or class using *Nehemiah Response: a coaching model* and *Relevant Discipleship Pathway™: a framework for intentional transformation that multiplies.* The coaching model and pathway books will immerse your group or class in the coaching approach and the discipleship pathway.

These three resources are available at Amazon.com. For information about quantity discounts, contact us at Relevant Ministry (contact@relevantministry.org).

76870164R00111

Made in the USA
Columbia, SC
27 September 2019